WORLD WAR II

WORLD

US TROOPS PARADING THROUGH PARIS, FRANCE, IN 1944

WAR II

SEAN CALLERY

SCHOLASTIC **discover more**™

WWII Heroes and Heroines

Download your free digital book and explore the extraordinary lives of war heroes and heroines. Meet code crackers, courageous soldiers and medics on the battlefield, and children caught up in a war-torn world.

Your digital book is very simple to use. Enter the code (bottom right) to download it to any Mac or PC. Open it in Adobe Reader, also free to download. Then you're all set!

WORLD
Heroes and Heroines

A digital companion to World Wa

Child heroes

All children in war-torn countries endured hardships, from lack of food to limited clothing and toys. In Europe, thousands of city children were evacuated—sent away to live with strangers in safer areas, sometimes even in different countries. Many children lost parents who died in battle. Many more lost their homes in bombing raids or became **refugees**. Sadly, countless children died, including more than a million children killed by the Nazis and their allies during the Holocaust.

About

1.5 million

Jewish children were killed by Nazis and their collaborators

A group of children awaiting **evacuation** from London, UK, in autumn 1939 say good-bye to their parents before boarding a train. They traveled far from home to stay with families who took care of them during the war. Some children stayed with their new families for the entire war. Others were very homesick and came back to face life in the **Blitz**.

Evacuees had a small list of possessions they could take with them, including a change of clothes and a parcel of food.

A luggage label tied to each child notified the new caregiver of the child's name and age.

Good-bye, Daddy
Many children thro... to face life without... their parents served... Sometimes their pa...

👁 Eyewitness account from an evacuee

📹 See inside Anne Frank's hideout

◎ **discover more**—Anne Frank

Hyperlinks

All of the pages in the digital book are hyperlinked. Click the colored buttons for more facts and pictures, video clips, personal accounts, and tips for using your digital book.

Death-defying deeds

Find out what it was like to live through an air raid, go undercover in enemy territory as a secret agent, and meet the people who risked their lives to save others.

"In spite of everything I still believe that people are really good at heart." —ANNE FRANK

digital book

The "Secret Annex" above 263 Prinsengracht, Amsterdam, was where Anne Frank hid and where she wrote her diary. Published as *The Diary of a Young Girl* in 1950, it gives a personal account of Nazi Germany's **persecution** of Jewish people during the Holocaust.

Child heroine [Anne Frank]

Anne was born Annelies Marie Frank on June 12, 1929, in Frankfurt am Main, Germany. She was the second daughter of Otto and Edith Frank. In 1933, the Franks moved to the Netherlands to leave behind the growing anti-Jewish atmosphere in Germany. Seven years later, German forces invaded the Netherlands.

On her 13th birthday, Anne's parents gave her a diary. A few weeks later, her sister, Margot, received a notice to report to a German labor camp. The next day—July 6, 1942—the family moved into a secret group of rooms next to Otto Frank's former office in Amsterdam. There, they and four other people hid for two years. Anne continued to write in her diary about her feelings, her family, and the plight of the **Nazis'** victims. Her entries came to a sudden halt when the Nazis discovered their hiding place on August 4, 1944. Anne and her family were taken to Auschwitz, a German **concentration camp** in Poland. In October, Anne and Margot were sent to another concentration camp, Bergen-Belsen, in Germany. In March 1945, Anne died there of **typhus** at the age of 15; Margot had died of the same disease a few days before. Just a few weeks later, the camp was liberated by the British army.

Anne Frank is shown here aged about 13, before she and her family went into hiding for two years.

🔖 *In spite of everything I still believe that people are really good at heart.* 🔖
—Anne Frank

🏠 HOME

Around the world . . .

» Teen survivor
Nazi collaborators also rounded up and killed thousands of Roma. Maria Sava Moise lived in Iasi, Romania, and was a teenager in 1941 when she and Iasi's other Roma were taken. She recalls the horror: "We were marched to a farm and left in open fields to die slowly." Maria's sister died, but her father, a soldier, rescued Maria and others on a troop train.

» Picture this
Keiji Nakazawa was six years old when the **atomic bomb** was dropped on Hiroshima, Japan, killing many thousands of people. Of his family, only Keiji and his

mother survived. Years later, he recorded his memories in manga (cartoon) form. His most famous books are *I Saw It* and *Hadashi no Gen (Barefoot Gen)*, about a six-year-old in the war.

» Scouts
Boy and girl scouts (Szare Szeregi) from all over Poland, some as young as ten years old, participated in the Warsaw Polish Uprising of 1944 to help free Warsaw from the occupying Nazis. Sadly, many were killed. Other scouts, such as brothers Zbik and Rys Jeleniewicz, became scout postmen, delivering newspapers and news in their community.

The Jeleniewicz brothers delivered newspapers to sympathizers in August 1944.

Child soldier

Children were often considered valuable assets in the war and used to fight the enemy, to help defend a city, or simply as human shields. Sometimes the young soldiers were treated well and made to feel powerful and brave so that they would be happy to follow their leaders' orders. In other cases, the children were forced to fight and would have been killed if they had refused.

Soviet army regiments accepted orphans, calling them "sons of the regiment." The children lived with the soldiers and fought alongside them, sometimes even earning medals for bravery in battle. There are no official records, but researchers claim that thousands of young soldiers (from 6 to 16 years of age) were employed on the front lines. Many carried arms, others delivered messages or helped medics.

In other countries, children willingly joined resistance movements to help defend their hometowns or fight back against occupying forces. In Poland, they played a role in the Warsaw Ghetto Uprising of 1943. The German army had crowded almost 500,000 Jewish people into an area of Warsaw called a ghetto. Conditions were appalling. Starting on April 19, the starved and weakened occupants of the ghetto—including many children—fought back to prevent the Nazis from taking them to the Treblinka extermination camp. Children across Poland joined renewed efforts in 1944 to free Warsaw from the Nazis in the Warsaw Polish Uprising.

25,000
child soldiers are estimated to have been engaged on the front lines in Russia

In-depth info
To discover even more, click the colored words to link to encyclopedia pages with in-depth articles on essential topics. Glossary entries explain difficult terms.

Consultant: Terry Charman, Senior Historian, Imperial War Museum London

Literacy Consultant: Barbara Russ, 21st Century Community Learning Center Director for Winooski (Vermont) School District

Project Editor: Clare Hibbert

Project Art Editor: Mark Lloyd

Designers: Clare Joyce, Silke Spingies

Art Director: Bryn Walls

US Editor: Esther Lin

Managing Editor: Miranda Smith

Managing Production Editor: Stephanie Engel

Cover Designer: Neal Cobourne

DTP: Sunita Gahir, John Goldsmid

Digital Photography Editor: Stephen Chin

Visual Content Project Manager: Diane Allford-Trotman

Executive Director of Photography, Scholastic: Steve Diamond

" There is no blinking at the fact that our people, our territory, and our interests are in grave danger "

—FRANKLIN D. ROOSEVELT, DECEMBER 8, 1941

Library of Congress Cataloging-in-Publication Data Available

ISBN 978-0-545-47975-2

10 9 8 7 6 5 4 3 2   13 14 15 16 17

Printed in Singapore   46
First edition, January 2013

Scholastic is constantly working to lessen the environmental impact of our manufacturing processes. To view our industry-leading paper procurement policy, visit www.scholastic.com/paperpolicy.

WOMAN WORKING ON A VENGEANCE DIVE-BOMBER, TENNESSEE, 1943

Contents

A show of strength 8
Destroyed cities 10

The path to war

Road to war 14
Rise of Nazi Germany 16
The Berlin Olympics 18
Ideologies 20
Blitzkrieg 22
Refugees 24
Theaters of war 26

Europe & the Atlantic war

War in Europe 30
Hitler blocked 32

The Blitz 34
Resistance 36
The eastern front 38
Stalingrad 40
The Holocaust 42
Remembered 44
Starve Britain 46
U-boat 48
Codes 50

War in the Pacific

The Pacific theater 54
Pearl Harbor 56
Culture during wartime 58
Women and the war 60
Wartime childhood 62
Sea battles 64

Jungle fighting 66
Guns 68
POWs 70
B-24 72
Island-hopping 74
The Battle of Iwo Jima 76

War in Africa & the Middle East

Africa and the Middle East 80
War in the desert 82
M4 Sherman 84
Spies and special ops 86
Victory in North Africa 88

The end of the war

Path to peace 92
D-Day 94
Battle of the Bulge 96
Berlin falls 98
Hiroshima 100
The war in numbers 102
The postwar world 104
Glossary 106
Index 109
Credits and acknowledgments 112

A show of strength

By 1944, the German army had installed a string of enormous guns, like this one, along France's Atlantic coast. They were put there to defend the territory that Germany had captured across Europe. By then, the most terrible war in history had also seen conflict in Africa, Asia, and the Pacific. Countries fought to protect the freedom of their people, lands, and ideas.

Destroyed cities

In World War II, families and children suffered as never before. Hundreds of cities and towns were turned to rubble as battles were fought in, around, and above them. This picture was taken in Saint-Lô, northern France, in July 1944; the scene was similar in Stalingrad, in the Soviet Union, or Warsaw, in Poland, or Dresden, in Germany.

The
tov

* What spectacle took place in Berlin in 1936?

* Who led Germany—and the world—into war?

* What was life like for wartime refugees?

path
war

Road to war [From 1918 to

In the 1930s, militaristic regimes ruled in Germany, Italy, and Japan. Their citizens wanted strong leaders to solve economic problems arising from a worldwide slump and, in Germany, hard conditions imposed by the peace treaties following World War I.

JAN. 1933
Adolf Hitler
Hitler, leader of the Nazi Party, seized power from President Paul von Hindenburg. Hitler was popular because he promised to make Germany great again. He immediately began to build up the country's army and weapons.

HITLER WITH HINDENBURG

JULY 1914–NOV. 1918
WWI
This appalling conflict in which 15 million died was a victory for Britain, France, Russia, and Italy over the German and Austro-Hungarian empires. The victors used the Treaty of Versailles to force Germany to disarm, give up lands, and pay vast sums of money.

ALLIED SOLDIERS FIGHTING IN THE TRENCHES

SEPT. 1931
Japan invaded Manchuria, on the east coast of China, to gain vital territory and minerals.

AUG. 1936
Hitler introduced military conscription—against the terms of the Treaty of Versailles, which had limited his army to 100,000 troops.

•1920•   •1930•

Dots represent yearly increases until 1939.

OCT. 1922
In Italy, Benito Mussolini, leader of the National Fascist Party, marched on Rome and seized power.

JAN. 1924
In the Communist Soviet Union (now Russia), Vladimir Lenin died. Joseph Stalin took control.

OCT. 1935
Eager to gain territory in Africa, Italy used powerful mustard gas to help it conquer Abyssinia (now Ethiopia).

MAR. 1936
When German troops entered the Rhineland, on the border with France, no one tried to stop them.

OCT. 1929
The crash
The collapse of the New York Stock Exchange on Wall Street triggered the Great Depression, an economic slump that spread across the Western world. Millions lost their jobs and savings, and Germany suffered badly.

CROWDS PANICKING ON WALL STREET

JULY 1936
Trouble in Spain
When the Spanish Civil War began, Hitler and Mussolini helped the nationalist general Francisco Franco to victory. The German air force carried out the first large-scale bombings of civilians and destroyed the Spanish town of Guernica in 1937.

FRANCISCO FRANCO
Dictator, Spain

In power:	1936–75
Party:	Nationalist

AUG. 1938
The Spitfire enters service
Britain began building large numbers of this speedy, single-seater fighter plane. War was clearly coming, and control of the skies would be vital to defend the island nation from attack.

PRIDE OF
THE RAF:
THE SPITFIRE

NOV. 9, 1938
Kristallnacht
The Nazi regime brutally oppressed political opponents and minorities, particularly the Jewish people. Kristallnacht ("Crystal Night") is named for all the shattered glass left on German streets after a night destroying Jewish property.

CLEANING UP AFTER
KRISTALLNACHT

MAR. 1938
Hitler took over the neighboring nation of Austria. Again, no one challenged him.

JULY 1937
Japan used conquered Manchuria as a base for its ruthless invasion of China.

APR. 1939
Italy invaded Albania. Mussolini was copying Hitler's aggressive empire-building strategy.

SEPT. 1939
France, Britain, and the Commonwealth countries Australia, New Zealand, South Africa, and Canada declared war on Germany. The US stayed neutral.

1939

NOV. 1936
Germany and Italy signed a treaty of friendship, known as the Rome-Berlin Axis.

Dots represent monthly increases during 1939.

FEB. 1939
Germany launched a massive battleship, the Bismarck, displaying to the world the power of its navy.

AUG. 1939
German-Soviet Pact
Germany and the Soviet Union agreed not to attack each other, and secretly divided Eastern Europe between them. Germany broke the terms of the Munich Pact and invaded Poland on September 1.

GERMAN TANKS IN POLAND

NEVILLE
CHAMBERLAIN
Prime minister, Britain
In power: 1937–40
Party: Conservative

SEPT. 1938
Munich Pact
Eager to avoid a war and to support an enemy of Communism, European leaders allowed Hitler to occupy part of Czechoslovakia. The British prime minister, Neville Chamberlain, called the deal "peace for our time."

38 million:
the number of gas masks given out in Britain
a year after the Munich Pact

The Treaty of Versailles (1919) saw the victors of World War I strip Germany of land and demand huge payments as punishment. This damaged the German economy, and unemployment rose. Adolf Hitler offered an answer, promising to create a new German empire.

Party membership

Germans believed that Hitler would make their country great again. When the Nazi Party gained power, it controlled who received the best jobs. To gain government employment, one had to join the party. Those who didn't became outsiders.

Play money

When the German reichsmark currency collapsed, children played with stacks of banknotes that had no value.

Bid for power

Hitler's National Socialist Party, often called the Nazi Party, tried to seize power in 1923. Hitler was found guilty of treason and spent eight months in jail. There he wrote *Mein Kampf* ("*My Struggle*") and outlined his belief that Germany must seize new lands.

Military beginnings

Born in 1889 in a German-speaking part of Austria, Hitler hoped to be an artist. But he always admired Germany and eagerly signed up to fight on its side in World War I (1914–18).

Worthless money

In 1923, the German monetary system fell apart. The United States aided its recovery with enormous loans. But in 1929, the US economy collapsed with the Wall Street Crash. The US government was forced to call in all of its loans. The resulting worldwide Great Depression hit Germany especially hard.

Nazi Germany: Time line

Sept. 1919 *The army sent Hitler, now a corporal, to spy on extremist groups. He joined the German Workers' Party, forerunner of the Nazi Party.*

July 29, 1921 *Hitler became the Nazi leader and took the title "Führer." His rousing speeches attracted large crowds.*

Nov. 9, 1923 *Hitler failed in an attempt to overthrow the government. At his trial, his speeches received a great deal of publicity.*

Apr. 4, 1925 *The Schutzstaffel (SS) was formed. It was led by Heinric. Himmler, who later ran the Gestapo, or secret police.*

Hitler takes over

In January 1933, after an election with no clear winner, German president Paul von Hindenburg appointed Hitler chancellor, leading a multiparty government.

But Hitler used emergency powers to take over running the state. When Hindenburg died in August 1934, Hitler became president.

Hitler Youth
German children had to join a Nazi youth organization. They were taught to love Germany and hate Jews and Communists.

The Third Reich

Hitler created jobs by strengthening the army and starting new building projects. He wanted to establish an empire known as the Third Reich (*Reich* means "empire"). The previous ones had been the Holy Roman Empire (800–1806) and the German Empire (1871–1918).

Technology
Hitler funded research on new military technologies. Scientist Wernher von Braun's work in the 1930s led to a pioneering rocket missile, the V-2.

Flag for the new empire
The German flag was black, red, and yellow. In 1935, a new flag combined the red, white, and black colors of the Second Reich, plus the Nazi swastika (see page 20).

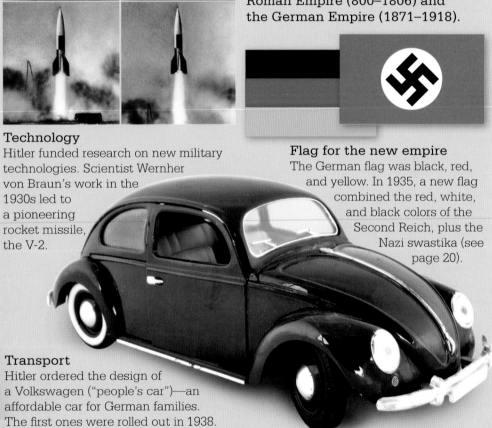

Transport
Hitler ordered the design of a Volkswagen ("people's car")—an affordable car for German families. The first ones were rolled out in 1938.

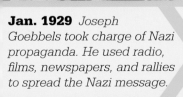

Jan. 1929 *Joseph Goebbels took charge of Nazi propaganda. He used radio, films, newspapers, and rallies to spread the Nazi message.*

Mar. 5, 1933 *The Nazis won 44 percent of votes in a general election. Hitler continued to eliminate all opposition and centralize power.*

Sept. 15, 1935 *Hitler passed new laws that made Jews second-class citizens. They no longer had the right to vote in elections.*

Mar. 7, 1936 *Hitler started reclaiming land for the Reich. He put troops in the Rhineland for the first time since World War I.*

The Berlin Olympics [Nazi

The 1936 Summer Olympics were held in Berlin, the capital of Germany. Nazi dictator Hitler used them to showcase the military efficiency of his nation. The 49 competing countries did not challenge Hitler then or in the years that followed, even when he invaded neighboring countries. No one wanted to provoke a war.

Jesse Owens

The hero of the Games was African American athlete Jesse Owens, who won 4 gold medals and broke 11 Olympic records. His triumphs included defeating German star athlete Lutz Long in the long jump. Hitler was furious that an "inferior" person had defeated a white person.

On the podium
At the medal ceremony, Long (right) gave a Nazi salute during the playing of the US national anthem.

Appeasing Hitler

The major European powers were worn out by war. Many thought that the reparations imposed on Germany in 1919 were harsh and that, like them, Hitler opposed Communism. They allowed Germany to invade Austria and, in late 1938, signed the Munich Pact.

Munich accord
Hitler and British prime minister Neville Chamberlain shake hands in Munich, 1938.

Czech invasion

The Munich Pact allowed Hitler to take over part of Czechoslovakia. The conquest of the rest of the country then became Hitler's goal. In 1939, German troops marched over the border. The other European powers suddenly realized that they could no longer trust Hitler.

Conquered city
The name of the Square of Liberty in the Czech city of Brno is changed to Adolf Hitler Square.

Nazi Germany: Time line

Mar. 7, 1936 *More than 32,000 German soldiers marched into the Rhineland, bordering France. They met no opposition.*

Nov. 25, 1936 *Germany and Japan signed the Anti-Comintern Pact against the Communist Soviet Union. Italy joined in 1937.*

Mar. 12, 1938 *Hitler entered Vienna, Austria, breaking the Treaty of Versailles. The other western powers took no action.*

Sept. 29, 1938 *Hitler promised not to invade other lands if he was given part of Czechoslovakia in the Munich Pact.*

One month

before the Games, top German high jumper Gretel Bergmann was dropped for being Jewish

Crowd-pleaser
Hitler used the Berlin Games to gain popularity in Germany and to promote his image around the world. Huge crowds showed their support with salutes and chants of *"Sieg Heil"* ("Hail to victory").

Mar. 16, 1939 *Germany occupied the rest of Czechoslovakia. Again, other western powers did nothing to stop him.*

Aug. 1939 *Germany and the Soviet Union signed a nonaggression pact. They agreed to share Poland between them.*

Sept. 1, 1939 *Assured of Italy's support, Germany invaded Poland. Britain and France responded by declaring war on Germany.*

More here
For key to symbols, see page 112

1936 Berlin Olympics
Nazi **Hitler** Jesse Owens
Anti-Comintern Pact
Czechoslovakia

***The Nazi Olympics:
Berlin 1936***
by Susan D. Bachrach

***Flying a Flag for
Hitler: My Childhood
in Nazi Germany***
by Elsbeth Emmerich

***Good-Bye Marianne:
A Story of Growing Up
in Nazi Germany***
by Irene N. Watts

Leni Riefenstahl's *Olympia* documents the 1936 Games; her ***Triumph of the Will*** shows Hitler's famous rally at Nuremberg in 1934.

Visit the **Olympic Stadium** in Berlin, Germany, now the home of soccer team Hertha BSC. It is also used for music and other sporting events.

appeasement: the act of making undue concessions to satisfy the demands of someone greedy for power.

Nazi: a member of Hitler's National Socialist Party in Germany, which promoted racist, authoritarian ideas.

Ideologies [Big ideas]

During the 1930s, a number of very different (and sometimes opposing) ideologies, or belief systems, were developed around the world. These differences eventually led to war.

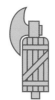

FASCES

Fascism

Fascism is named after the fasces, an ancient Roman symbol of authority and power. Fascists value leadership and expect a dictator, or powerful ruler, to tell the people what to do.

Key points

Origins:	Fascist ideas spread from France in the 1880s
Children were taught:	The state is best
Led by:	A dictator, so that there are no disputes
Most influential group:	The military, to protect the state and suppress opposition
Opposed to:	Communism

Fascist Italy

BENITO MUSSOLINI

Lived:	July 29, 1883– April 28, 1945
Led:	Italy (1922–45)
Nickname:	Il Duce ("the Leader")

Italy and Benito Mussolini
In 1922, Mussolini and his followers, the Blackshirts, marched on Rome to take power. He became dictator in 1927.

SWASTIKA

Nazism

Nazis were Fascists who also believed in the superiority of Aryans (white, non-Jewish people, ideally blond with blue eyes). They thought they had the right to enslave "inferior" peoples. Their symbol was the swastika.

Key points

Origins:	Hitler put forward the founding ideas of Nazism in his book *Mein Kampf* (1925)
Children were taught:	The Aryan race is supreme
Led by:	A dictator
Most influential group:	The military, to expand the German state and form a new empire called the Third Reich
Opposed to:	Jews, nonwhites, and Communism

Nazi Germany

Germany and Adolf Hitler
Even though he was Austrian, Hitler believed that the Aryan master race should build a new German empire.

ADOLF HITLER

Lived:	April 20, 1889– April 30, 1945
Led:	Germany (1933–45)
Nickname:	The Führer ("the Leader")

"**What we have to fight for is . . . the freedom and independence of the Fatherland**"
—ADOLF HITLER

"**The people do not know what they want. . . . I have stopped the talk and the nonsense. I am a man of action**"
—BENITO MUSSOLINI

Two dictators
Hitler (center) and Mussolini (left) were allies but did not fully trust each other.

Communism

HAMMER AND SICKLE

According to Communism, all property and businesses should be owned by the people. Its hammer and sickle symbol represents industry and farming, showing that factory workers and farmers can work together.

Key points

Origins:	Karl Marx developed the idea of Communism in his manifesto in 1848
Children were taught:	No one has his or her own private property
Led by:	The Communist Party (often led by a dictator)
Most influential group:	Party leaders
Opposed to:	Capitalism (a free economy)

Communist Soviet Union

Soviet Union and Joseph Stalin
The Soviet Union (or USSR) formed in 1922. From 1924, Joseph Stalin began to take over.

JOSEPH STALIN

Lived:	December 18,1878– March 5, 1953
Led:	Soviet Union (1924–53)
Nickname:	Vozhd ("the Boss")

> ## "From each according to his ability, to each according to his needs"
> —JOSEPH STALIN

Democracy

BALLOT BOX

In democracies, people vote every few years for political representatives. Those with the most votes make, pass, or veto laws. Everyone has the right to express his or her own opinions.

Key points

Origins:	The ancient Greeks were the first known to elect leaders
Children were taught:	Freedom and equality are vital
Led by:	A president or prime minister from an elected party
Most influential groups:	Lawmakers and voters
Opposed to:	Dictatorships

Democracy and the world
By the 1930s, there were many democratic countries, such as the United States, led by President Roosevelt, and the United Kingdom.

FRANKLIN D. ROOSEVELT

Lived:	January 30, 1882– April 12, 1945
Led:	United States (1933–45)
Nickname:	FDR

> ## "As I would not be a slave, so I would not be a master. This expresses my idea of democracy"
> —ABRAHAM LINCOLN

Militarism
Japan was led by Emperor Hirohito from 1929, but its real rulers were the heads of the army. Under this strong military rule, Japan wanted to expand into China and Southeast Asia, conquering European colonies to build its own empire. Japan's slogan was "Asia for the Asians."

Rising sun
This military flag shows the rays from Japan's rising sun symbol, spreading out to reach new territory.

Fighting for new lands
Eager to expand, Japan had fought and won against the Russians in Manchuria and Korea, from 1904 to 1905, and went to war with China in 1937.

Blitzkrieg [Lightning war]

Germany conquered Poland in September 1939 with blitzkrieg ("lightning war") tactics. After an eight-month delay in military action—the "Phony War"—the Germans suddenly swept across Europe.

Military buildup

Germany's quick victories were the result of years of preparation. From 1933 to 1939, Hitler increased the German army tenfold, to 1 million soldiers. His air force grew from 36 to 8,250 planes, and his navy from 30 to 95 warships.

123 TANKS

Panzer (tank) division

A German tank division was made up of panzers and their crews, support staff, and equipment. The exact numbers varied, but a typical tank division in 1940 included:

1,402 TRUCKS

561 PASSENGER VEHICLES

421 ARMORED VEHICLES

1,280 MOTORCYCLES

394 OFFICERS

1,962 NONCOMMISSIONED OFFICERS

9,321 SOLDIERS

Germany

May 1940	Germany	Allies
Divisions	154	144
Armored vehicles	4,000	4,000
Fighter planes	1,100	1,100
Bombers	1,100	400
Dive-bombers	400	0

Plans for expansion

Adolf Hitler planned to take over countries bordering Germany and use their "inferior" citizens as slave labor. He expected Britain to negotiate for peace.

Opposing forces

The German army had more up-to-date equipment than the Allied forces of Britain, France, and Belgium did. The Allies' resources were also spread very thin.

INVADED:
MAY 10, 1940
SURRENDERED:
MAY 28, 1940

BRUSSELS

BELGIUM

Eben-Emael

Belgium

After overpowering the 630 soldiers defending the strategic fortress of Eben-Emael, German forces rolled across Belgium. The capital, Brussels, fell in May.

9

55

630

Capturing Eben-Emael

Gliders landed 55 paratroopers armed with flamethrowers to take this key Belgian fortress.

Ardennes Forest

PARIS

FRANCE

INVADED:
MAY 12, 1940
SURRENDERED:
JUNE 22, 1940

France

German tanks passed through the hilly, dense Ardennes Forest—to the surprise of the French. Pushing over roads clogged with terrified refugees, the invaders reached Paris on June 14.

French prisoners

1,575,600 prisoners were taken to Germany to work as slave labor.

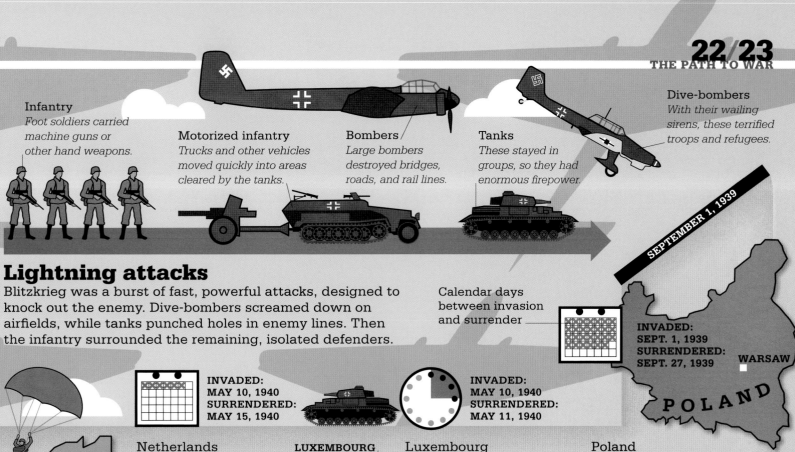

Infantry
Foot soldiers carried machine guns or other hand weapons.

Motorized infantry
Trucks and other vehicles moved quickly into areas cleared by the tanks.

Bombers
Large bombers destroyed bridges, roads, and rail lines.

Tanks
These stayed in groups, so they had enormous firepower.

Dive-bombers
With their wailing sirens, these terrified troops and refugees.

Lightning attacks

Blitzkrieg was a burst of fast, powerful attacks, designed to knock out the enemy. Dive-bombers screamed down on airfields, while tanks punched holes in enemy lines. Then the infantry surrounded the remaining, isolated defenders.

SEPTEMBER 1, 1939

Calendar days between invasion and surrender

INVADED: SEPT. 1, 1939
SURRENDERED: SEPT. 27, 1939

WARSAW

POLAND

INVADED: MAY 10, 1940
SURRENDERED: MAY 15, 1940

INVADED: MAY 10, 1940
SURRENDERED: MAY 11, 1940

Netherlands
German paratroopers were dropped in to smooth the way for the ground forces. After the Luftwaffe (air force) bombing of Rotterdam left 80,000 people homeless, the Dutch surrendered, fearing more attacks.

AMSTERDAM
ROTTERDAM
NETHERLANDS

LUXEMBOURG
LUXEMBOURG

Luxembourg
With no army, neutral Luxembourg didn't stand a chance. It took just three hours for three German panzer divisions to rumble the 30 miles (48 km) across this tiny country.

Poland
Poland could not defend its long border against the Reich. Hitler had a pact to share Poland with the Soviet Union; Stalin invaded on September 17. Warsaw surrendered on September 27.

1,308

Deadly drop
The Germans dropped 1,308 bombs on the Dutch port of Rotterdam.

940,000 remained until 1945

24,600 prisoners died

71,000 escaped

320,000

220,000

Released to Vichy regime (see right)

Released for disability or sickness

Paris, France
Hitler kept the capital under German control but allowed southern France to govern itself until November 11, 1942, when Vichy France was occupied.

47,000

Refugees
47,000 people fled from Luxembourg to France. They didn't realize that the Germans were heading there, too.

German 8,082
GERMAN
POLISH

Polish 95,000

DEAD: 103,082

German 27,278

Polish 130,000

WOUNDED: 157,278

Heavy Polish losses
In the invasion, 12 Poles died for every 1 German. Nearly 5 times as many Polish people were wounded.

"The small countries are simply smashed up, one by one, like matchwood"

—WINSTON CHURCHILL'S MESSAGE TO FRANKLIN D. ROOSEVELT, MAY 15, 1940

Refugees

The fighting and the threat of Nazi rule terrified millions of people who were in the path of the invasion. Many, like this French family, packed as many possessions as they could and fled on the dusty roads. Leaving behind homes, jobs, and normal life, refugees faced hardships and danger. Many were even attacked by German dive-bombers.

Theaters of war [Worldwide]

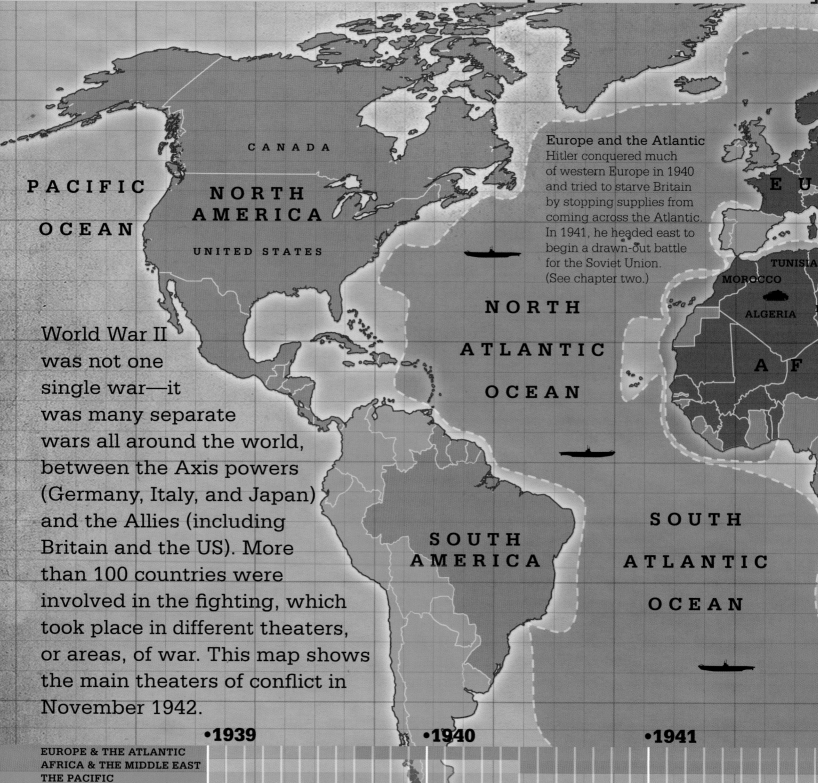

CANADA

PACIFIC OCEAN

NORTH AMERICA

UNITED STATES

Europe and the Atlantic
Hitler conquered much
of western Europe in 1940
and tried to starve Britain
by stopping supplies from
coming across the Atlantic.
In 1941, he headed east to
begin a drawn-out battle
for the Soviet Union.
(See chapter two.)

E U

TUNISIA

MOROCCO

ALGERIA

L

A F

NORTH ATLANTIC OCEAN

World War II
was not one
single war—it
was many separate
wars all around the world,
between the Axis powers
(Germany, Italy, and Japan)
and the Allies (including
Britain and the US). More
than 100 countries were
involved in the fighting, which
took place in different theaters,
or areas, of war. This map shows
the main theaters of conflict in
November 1942.

SOUTH AMERICA

SOUTH ATLANTIC OCEAN

•1939

•1940

•1941

EUROPE & THE ATLANTIC
AFRICA & THE MIDDLE EAST
THE PACIFIC

Key events of the war
The Axis powers advanced
from 1939 to 1942 but were
slowly defeated, at a
cost of millions of lives.

1940 *The British
air victory in the
Battle of Britain put
a stop to Hitler's
western advance.*

1941 *Japan's attempt to
destroy the US Pacific Fleet
in the naval base at Pearl
Harbor, HI, brought the
United States into the war.*

MAP KEY
1. Ireland 2. Britain
3. Portugal 4. Spain
5. France 6. Belgium
7. Netherlands 8. Luxembourg
9. Switzerland 10. Italy
11. Sardinia 12. Germany
13. Denmark 14. Norway
15. Sweden 16. Finland
17. Estonia 18. Latvia
19. Lithuania 20. East Prussia
21. Poland 22. Czechoslovakia
23. Austria 24. Hungary
25. Romania 26. Yugoslavia
27. Albania 28. Greece
29. Bulgaria 30. Turkey

SOVIET UNION

Stalingrad

PACIFIC

OCEAN

SOVIET UNION

MANCHURIA

ASIA

Toyko

CHINA

JAPAN

Midway

MIDDLE
EAST

EGYPT

SAUDI
ARABIA

INDIA

BURMA

The Pacific
Japan attacked China
in 1937, then more Asian
and Pacific lands in 1941,
forcing the US into the war. Early
successes in 1942 were countered
by a long, hard fight until 1945.
(See chapter three.)

SUDAN

PHILIPPINES

ABYSSINIA
(ETHIOPIA)

Pearl Harbor

MALAYA

KENYA

SINGAPORE

BORNEO

**Africa and the
Middle East**
Italy attacked in Africa in
1940 and was joined by German
forces in 1941. One target was
the valuable oil fields of the
Middle East, then controlled by
Britain. Axis forces were pushed
back in 1943. (See chapter four.)

SUMATRA

NEW GUINEA

SOLOMON
ISLANDS

INDIAN OCEAN

AUSTRALIA

SOUTH
FRICA

MAP KEY
Allied powers   Under Axis control
Neutral countries

NEW ZEALAND

942   •1943   •1944   •1945

1942 *The US naval victory
at the Battle of Midway
stopped Japanese advances.
Then the Allies began the
long push toward Tokyo.*

1943 *On the eastern
front, Germany was
forced into retreat after
losing at Stalingrad in
the Soviet Union.*

1945 *Allied advances from
both east and west forced a
German surrender on May 7.
Atomic bombs helped end the
war with Japan on August 14.*

Europ
Atlant

* Which air attacks reduced British cities to rubble?

* Why did some Jewish families go into hiding?

* Which were the deadliest WWII submarines?

e & the

ic war

If Hitler wanted to invade Britain, he would first have to gain control of the skies over southern England. So the Luftwaffe sent its speedy Me 109 fighter planes to face British Spitfires and Hurricanes. The Battle of Britain was fought from July 10 to October 31, 1940.

Hurricane specifications	
Top speed	325 mph (523 kph)
Range	600 mi. (965 km)
Maximum altitude	34,000 ft. (10,365 m)
Wingspan	40 ft. (12 m)
Armament	8 machine guns
Number built	14,533

Hood
This was built from the newly invented bulletproof material Perspex.

Machine guns
The pilot fired the four guns by pushing a button in short bursts.

Tail fin
The rounded tail fin and large rudder allowed the plane to make tight turns.

Tail wheel
This wheel did not tuck in during flight.

Dogfights
When German planes crossed the English Channel to attack British radar stations and airfields, Royal Air Force (RAF) pilots took off to intercept them. Groups of planes had deadly dogfights, performing desperate corkscrew turns and dives. Each tried to get behind an enemy plane and fire a blast of bullets or shells to rip it apart and send it spiraling downward.

Propeller
Three metal blades sliced through the air.

Wing
The aluminum covering was lightweight but strong.

Hawker Hurricane
Hurricanes claimed more than half of the German planes shot down in the Battle of Britain. They could be rearmed, refueled, and ready to return to the skies in just nine minutes.

Scramble!
Between fights, pilots tried to rest. Then the next warning would come in, and they would "scramble," running to their planes. Sometimes they flew five missions in a single day. Their biggest fear was being burned alive in a shot-down plane.

Ready to fly
A British pilot wore leather headgear that had a built-in oxygen mask and radio.

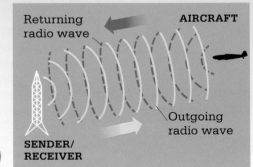

Returning radio wave   AIRCRAFT

Outgoing radio wave

SENDER/ RECEIVER

How radar helped
Radar sends out radio waves that bounce back off objects such as planes. This vital tool allowed the British to detect enemy planes before they came into sight.

Me 109 specifications

Top speed	398 mph (640 kph)
Range	530 mi. (850 km)
Maximum altitude	39,370 ft. (11,880 m)
Wingspan	32.5 ft. (10 m)
Armament	2 machine guns, 1 cannon
Number built	32,984

"Never in the field of human conflict was so much owed by so many to so few" —WINSTON CHURCHILL

Pilot
The pilot's heated flying suit plugged into the cockpit.

Frame
The plane was made of thin, light metal to reduce drag.

Front cannon
Shells were fired through the propeller.

Fuel tank
This held enough fuel for a flight just over an hour long.

Wing
The wings were thin and light, with special slats that provided more control during dives.

Engine
The fuel-injected engine was better at handling dives than that of a British plane.

Messerschmitt Bf 109
Known as the Me 109 for short, this sleek fighter could climb and dive faster than its British rivals, but it did not turn as well. The Luftwaffe relied on about 33,000 Me 109s.

Wing gun
Bullets for this gun were fed from the fuselage, to keep the wings light.

Dunkirk
In late May 1940, the Germans had the British, French, and Belgian forces pinned down and at their mercy on the French coast, near Dunkirk. A rescue fleet was sent across the English Channel before Hitler had a chance to attack. The 861 boats ferried 338,000 troops back to Britain. They had to abandon their equipment—but they were safe!

Little ships
Troops waded through choppy waters in their heavy uniforms to reach their rescuers. Small fishing and sailing boats shuttled the men to destroyers and other large craft.

The Blitz

For eight months after September 7, 1940, the Germans rained down bombs on Britain's cities. The Blitz left 43,000 people dead and 250,000 homeless. A night for a typical family might have gone like this:

6:00 PM — Blackout curtains are closed so that lights inside the house won't help bombers find a target.

6:30 PM — The family puts an emergency bag by the door. It contains a flashlight, candles, matches, blankets, ration books, gas masks, and ID cards.

8:00 PM — The air-raid siren wails: Radar has detected bombers over the English Channel.

8:10 PM — The family leaves the doors of the house open, to limit the effects of a blast. In the yard, they hurry down the steps of an air-raid shelter.

8:20 PM — Antiaircraft guns clatter at the bombers, aided by searchlights. The family hears the whistle of falling high-explosive bombs and the wail of fire engines.

10:30 PM — The next wave of planes releases high explosives, and the shelter rattles with each blast.

5:00 AM — The two-minute "all clear" siren sounds. The family finds their house unscathed—this time.

7:00 AM — The cleanup begins: sweeping glass, digging out bodies, and tending to the injured, while children rush to add to their shrapnel collections.

177,000
people slept on underground train platforms

The eastern front [Attack

On June 22, 1941, Hitler switched his attack from western to eastern Europe. He broke his peace pact with Stalin and invaded the Soviet Union with a force of 4 million troops. Hitler wanted to control the country's resources, rule its "inferior" peoples, defeat Communism, and kill Russian Jews. However, just six months later, the Germans were forced to retreat outside Moscow.

"It is the Führer's unshakable decision to raze Moscow and Leningrad to the ground"
—GERMAN SUPREME COMMAND, 1941

The invasion
The Germans advanced quickly, thanks to their state-of-the-art weapons. In just three months, they had killed or captured 3 million of the poorly equipped Soviet troops.

Operation Barbarossa
Hitler's plan was to capture and occupy the Soviet Union in the summer, when travel was easy on dry roads. Targets were major cities, oil fields, coalfields, and farms that could supply the Third Reich with fuel and food.

LENINGRAD
Sept. 8, 1941

MOSCOW
Oct. 13, 1941

RUSSIA

GERMAN ATTACKS

STALINGRAD
Aug. 23, 1942

Divided attack
Germany pushed forward toward the key cities of Leningrad, Moscow, and Stalingrad. Its forces were spread too thinly to conquer them.

on the Red Army]

Turning the tide

The Soviet Union's Red Army fought out of pride for their country—and fear. Stalin had ordered that those who deserted or surrendered would be shot, and their families punished. Slowly, the Soviets pushed the Germans back.

Supplying the army
Stalin moved munitions factories east, away from the fighting. The laborers worked grueling 18-hour shifts to keep the army supplied.

Rifle power

Hidden Soviet snipers could fire on enemy soldiers up to 1,200 feet (365 m) away. They worked in pairs. One acted as a lookout, and the other fired shots. Then they swapped.

Girl power
About 2,000 Red Army snipers were young women.

Weapon of choice
The Mosin-Nagant 1891/30 was the most often used Soviet sniper rifle.

Telescopic sight
This sight made the target appear about four times nearer.

Front sight
This sight helped the sniper line up his or her target more accurately.

Trigger
Pulling and releasing this fired the rifle.

Magazine
The ammunition cartridge went here.

Stalingrad

The Battle of Stalingrad, which began in the summer of 1942, was fought in a ruined city through the freezing winter. The Soviet victory, at the terrible cost of 490,000 Soviet and German lives, marked the first time Hitler's forces had to retreat.

AUG. 23 — Luftwaffe bombs turned much of the city to rubble and killed around 47,000 people. Some women and children were evacuated, but Stalin wanted Stalingrad's civilians to stay and fight.

SEPT. 13 — German troops reached the city center. Snipers were as useful as tanks in combat, because the battle was fought street by street and house by house.

NOV. 19 — 1 million Red Army troops began to encircle and bombard the Germans.

NOV. 23 — 275,000 German soldiers and 50,000 Soviet civilians were trapped for the winter. Vital supplies of food, fuel, and ammunition had to be dropped into the city by plane. Many people died from starvation, frostbite, or disease.

JAN. 1943 — The Soviets captured two key German airfields, preventing the delivery of crucial supplies.

JAN. 31 — The 91,000 Germans still alive surrendered and were taken prisoner. Only 10,000 Soviet civilians survived. These included 904 children, only 9 of whom ever found their parents again.

FEB. 2 — The German prisoners were marched east to Siberia. Tens of thousands died on the journey.

99%

of Stalingrad's buildings were destroyed in the siege

The Holocaust [The Final

When the Nazis came to power, more than 9 million Jewish people were living across Europe. In eastern Europe, they spoke Yiddish, and Yiddish culture thrived. Throughout Europe, they were successful in every walk of life. But anti-Semitism was common, and Hitler and the Nazis were able to implement a plan of genocide, or mass murder.

90% of Polish Jews were killed in the Holocaust

Nazi camps

Starting in 1933, violence toward Jews intensified. The Nazis established concentration camps and forced-labor camps to detain Jews and others considered a danger to the regime. Across Europe, Jews were herded into areas called ghettos, to control them and prepare them for the camps.

Hidden
Some Jewish families—including, famously, the family of Anne Frank—tried to hide. This hiding place is in Haarlem, the Netherlands.

The Final Solution

The Final Solution, the plan to exterminate the Jewish people, entered its deadliest phase in 1941. In Russia, more than 1 million Jews were rounded up and shot. In 1942, extermination camps were used to kill millions of Jews and other "inferior" people, such as Communists, Roma (Gypsies), and homosexuals. Jews were herded like cattle onto trains and transported to the camps to be gassed to death.

Yellow star
This patch identified its wearer as Jewish.

A culture disappears
The Jewish population of Europe fell shockingly because of Nazi repression and killings.

Jewish populations in Europe		
	Pre–Final Solution population	Killed in Final Solution
Poland	3,300,000	3,000,000
Soviet Union	2,850,000	1,252,000
Hungary	650,000	450,000
Romania	600,000	300,000
Baltic countries	253,000	228,000
Germany and Austria	240,000	210,000

Solution]

Rising up

By spring 1943, with many of their relatives and friends already sent to the death camps, Jewish people in the Warsaw ghetto launched an uprising against the Nazis. But it was a hopeless fight.

Eyewitness

NAME: Jürgen Stroop

DATE: 1943

LOCATION: Warsaw, Poland

DETAILS: Stroop was a loyal Nazi who joined Hitler's personal guard unit, the Waffen-SS. He held the rank of major general at the time he was sent to Poland, on April 17, 1943, to deal with the Warsaw Ghetto Uprising.

❝ On April 23 . . . [we were ordered] to complete the combing out of the Warsaw ghetto with the greatest severity and relentless tenacity. I therefore decided to destroy the entire Jewish residential area by setting every block on fire. ❞

More here

For key to symbols, see page 112

Survivors: True Stories of Children in the Holocaust
by Allan Zullo and Mara Bovsun

I Have Lived a Thousand Years: Growing Up in the Holocaust
by Livia Bitton-Jackson

The Diary of a Young Girl
by Anne Frank

See the collections at the **United States Holocaust Memorial Museum**, Washington, D.C., and the **Jewish Museum**, New York City, NY.

In the Netherlands, visit homes where Jews hid: the **Anne Frank House** and the **Corrie ten Boom Museum**.

Auschwitz-Birkenau Memorial is on the site of the concentration camp in Poland.

anti-Semitism: prejudice against or hatred of Jews.

concentration camp: a large compound where civilians, especially Jews, were kept in very harsh conditions. In some camps, also known as extermination or death camps, the prisoners were deliberately killed.

genocide: the systematic murder of many people from the same racial or cultural group.

ghetto: a section of a city, often a highly populated slum area, where Jews were made to live by the Nazis during World War II.

Prewar life

This picture shows Jewish children in the city of Lodz, Poland, in 1930. Their parents may have worked in the textile or construction industries. They lived ordinary lives: attending public schools, playing sports, and going to Yiddish theaters. The Lodz Jewish community, numbering more than 230,000, was completely wiped out during the Holocaust.

Remembered [Holocaust

The Nazis and their allies murdered 1.5 million children in death camps in less than four years. Most children arrived with relatives, often with their whole families. Nearly all those who were under ten years old were killed on arrival. The rest were put to work, often dying from disease or starvation or in random killings. Some of the children's names and the ages at which they died are printed here.

Eyewitness

"Most people who entered through the gates of Auschwitz-Birkenau were confronted with an immediate 'selection'; either to be admitted to the camp or to be killed by gas on arrival."

NAME: Kitty Hart-Moxon
LOCATION: Poland
DETAILS: Born into a Jewish family, Kitty Hart-Moxon survived a ghetto; the massacre of Jews at Belzec, Poland; and prison. In 1943, she was sent to the Auschwitz concentration camp. In 1945, as the Germans retreated, she and hundreds of other women were forcibly marched through Germany and Czechoslovakia. Most died on the journey. She was freed by American soldiers and went to live in England.

❝ Most people who entered through the gates of Auschwitz-Birkenau were confronted with an immediate 'selection'; either to be admitted to the camp or to be killed by gas on arrival. We were marched to be stripped, shaved of all hair, and tattooed on our left forearms. From then on we had no names. I was now number 39934 and my mother, 39933.

There was no water to wash [with] or drink, and no lavatories. The small bread ration was handed out after evening roll call and the camp soup, at midday. It would not sustain life for very long.

For many months I worked in dozens of work groups: loading dead bodies, digging trenches, or working in potato fields, which enabled me to smuggle some potatoes back into the camp.

There was an epidemic of typhus. Most people did not survive when they fell ill, as treatment was nonexistent. But I was taken to my mother, who looked after me and hid me during the daily selections for the gas chambers.

We witnessed the killing of more than half a million people. We girls could not take in what was happening—even though we heard the screams as people were dying. But it sank in eventually when we saw the people disappear before our eyes, never to be seen again, except for the piles of belongings left behind. ❞

"I believe in the Sun,
even when it is not shining.
And I believe in love,
even when there's no one there.
And I believe in God,
even when he is silent.

May there someday be sunshine.
May there someday be happiness.
May there someday be love.
May there someday be peace."

—CARVED ON A WALL BY AN UNKNOWN
VICTIM OF THE HOLOCAUST

Codes [Top secret]

Anyone can tune in to radio messages, so important ones were encrypted, or put into a code or cipher. The Allies' ability to break German and Japanese codes and ciphers gave them a vital advantage.

daisy
food
p y y n

Code
Entire words or phrases are changed to new words, symbols, or letters.

Original (plain text)

Cipher
Each letter is changed. Here, letters have been moved ten places ahead in the alphabet.

Cracking Enigma

The Germans invented a cipher machine called Enigma. They changed their ciphers daily and were convinced that they were unbreakable—but they were wrong. Helped by the Polish Cipher Bureau, the British cracked Enigma.

Letter window
This showed the setting of each rotor when the cipher was changed.

Rotors
These changed each letter as it was typed in.

Keyboard
This was where the plain-text message was typed in, one letter at a time.

ALAN TURING
Mathematician

Lived: June 23, 1912– June 7, 1954

Famous for: Building the first computer to help crack Enigma

Bletchley Park
The 2001 film *Enigma* was about Alan Turing and his team at Bletchley Park, England. They first cracked an Enigma message in 1940.

M 3097

Ticker-tape secrets

Both sides used special teleprinters, which turned text into a cipher and printed it out as a set of punched holes on tape.

1 A message is typed in plain text for a teleprinter machine to encrypt as a cipher.

2 The machine punches holes into ticker tape, which is fed into a special radio transmitter.

3 The receiving teleprinter machine prints out the received encrypted message as punched tape.

4 The message is deciphered using the same cipher settings, so it can be read as plain text.

MESSAGE ENCRYPTED, READY TO SEND

MESSAGE RECEIVED, READY TO DECIPHER

Enigma
The machine needed two people to work it. One typed the message, one letter at a time. The other read out each new letter that lit up on the lamp board cover, as the plain text became a cipher to be sent.

Lamp board cover
The letters here lit up to show the new encrypted message.

Plug board
Wires here changed some of the letters again, making the cipher even more complicated.

Dots and dashes

Developed in the 19th century, Morse code represents the letters of the alphabet with sequences of dots and dashes. It was used throughout the war.

MORSE SIGNALING LAMP WITH GREEN AND RED FILTERS

TELEGRAPH KEY FOR SENDING MORSE ELECTRONICALLY

Sending Morse code
Signalers sent messages over long distances in the form of electronic pulses along telegraph wires, and over short distances as flashes of light.

Japanese cipher

William F. Friedman of the US Signals Intelligence Service (SIS) looked for patterns in Japanese coded messages. Thanks to his work, the SIS cracked the Purple cipher in 1940. The Japanese never knew their security was breached.

Wrecked plane
In April 1943, top Japanese admiral Yamamoto Isoroku died after his plane was shot down. The US had deciphered his travel plans.

More here

For key to symbols, see page 112

code cipher **Purple cipher**
Alan Turing **Enigma**
William F. Friedman

The Cracking Codebook: How to Make It, Break It, Hack It, Crack It
by Simon Singh

Mysterious Messages: A History of Codes and Ciphers
by Gary Blackwood

Enigma (2001) is based on the story of the Bletchley Park code crackers.

Visit the **National Cryptologic Museum**, in Fort Meade, MD. Exhibits include a working German Enigma machine.

Bletchley Park is a museum on the site of the British code-breaking center and is home to the **National Museum of Computing**.

Practice writing messages in a shift cipher. Replace each letter with a letter a set number of places ahead in the alphabet.

War i
Pac

* Who masterminded the Pearl Harbor attack?

* Where did soldiers battle knee-deep in mud?

* What was so special about the B-24?

n the
ific

The Pacific theater [Total

The Japanese captured territory in Southeast Asia, as well as many Pacific islands, before setting up defensive bases across the area. But their failure to knock out the US Navy turned the hope for new territory into a disaster as the US fought back.

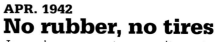

APR. 1942
No rubber, no tires
Japan's conquests gave it control of Asia's natural rubber, which deprived the United States of this vital material, used for tires and other essential equipment. US scientists developed synthetic rubber from petroleum just before the natural rubber ran out.

US MILITARY JEEP

YAMAMOTO ISOROKU

Japanese navy

Lived:	1884–1943
Rank in 1941:	Commander of the Combined Fleet

DEC. 1941
Pearl Harbor
Admiral Yamamoto planned Japan's surprise attack on the US Pacific Fleet's base at Pearl Harbor. It was meant to keep the US from interfering with Japanese expansion. Four of the eight battleships in the harbor were sunk.

FEB. 15, 1942
Japan captured the British colony of Singapore.

•1941   19

SEPT. 1940
Japan occupied French Indochina and became an ally of Germany and Italy.

JULY 1941
The US and Britain blocked all trade with Japan, and the US stopped supplying Japan with oil.

DEC. 1941
The US declared war on Japan. Germany and Italy declared war on the US.

DEC. 1941
Japan attacked Malaya and the Philippines to control the South China Sea.

APR. 9, 1942
Japan captured the Philippines, preventing US planes from using it as a base.

JUNE 1942
The US won the Battle of Midway, badly damaging the Japanese fleet.

AUG. 1942
US troops landed in the Solomon Islands.

MAR. 1942
Internment
After the Pearl Harbor attack, 110,000 Japanese Americans living across the US were forced to live behind barbed wire, in internment camps. Two-thirds were citizens born in the US. Congress apologized for this in 1988.

JAPANESE AMERICAN CHILDREN

APR. 18, 1942
Doolittle raid
The first US bomb attack on the Japanese capital, Tokyo, was planned and led by veteran pilot James "Jimmy" Doolittle. It did little damage, but this aerial return strike on Japan was a big victory for US morale and propaganda.

JAMES DOOLITTLE

US Air Force

Lived:	1896–1993
Rank in 1942:	Lieutenant colonel

MAY 1942
Battle of the Coral Sea

US ships intercepted a Japanese fleet aiming to invade New Guinea and the Solomon Islands. For four days, each side sent planes to drop bombs and torpedoes. There was no outright winner, but Japan's losses were greater.

USS *LEXINGTON*, SINKING IN THE CORAL SEA

OCT. 23–26, 1944
Leyte Gulf

A series of massive battles was fought in the waters of Leyte Gulf, near the Philippines. The US victory cut off the supply route from mainland Japan to its forces in Southeast Asia, a plan masterminded by Admiral Nimitz.

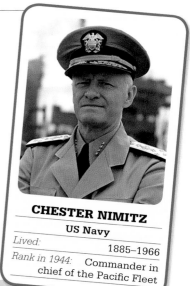

CHESTER NIMITZ
US Navy

Lived: 1885–1966
Rank in 1944: Commander in chief of the Pacific Fleet

JAN. 1943
At the Casablanca Conference, Churchill and Roosevelt agreed that they should insist on unconditional surrender from the Axis powers.

NOV. 1943
US landings on Bougainville, in the Solomon Islands, isolated Japanese forces and destroyed some of their key bases.

JUNE 19–20, 1944
Japan lost 3 carriers and 426 of its 473 operational aircraft in the Battle of the Philippine Sea.

Dots represent yearly increases.

APR. 12, 1945
President Roosevelt died and was replaced by his vice president, Harry S. Truman.

• 1944   • 1945

MAR. 1945
A US air raid set Tokyo on fire. At least 83,000 people died, and 1.5 million lost their homes. US troops also captured Iwo Jima.

FEB. 1943
War production

The US economy was set up for war. Car factories switched to building military vehicles. Millions of women joined the workforce, recruited by the newly created War Manpower Commission.

A RIVETER AT WORK ON A BOMBER IN A TEXAS FACTORY

APR. 1944
Battle of Imphal-Kohima

Battles at Imphal and Kohima, in India, turned back the Japanese invasion of Southeast Asia. Now Allied planes could fly from the area to attack the Japanese, who began to retreat through Burma.

CLEARING THE ROAD BETWEEN IMPHAL AND KOHIMA OF JAPANESE SOLDIERS

297,199:
the number of military aircraft built in the United States during the war

Pearl Harbor

On December 7, 1941, the Japanese attacked Pearl Harbor, on the Hawaiian island of Oahu. They hoped to wipe out the US Pacific Fleet, most of which was docked there. The surprise attack brought the United States into the war.

6:10 AM — 183 planes took off from 6 Japanese aircraft carriers in the ocean 230 miles (370 km) north of the target. There were 51 dive-bombers, 49 bombers, 40 torpedo bombers, and 43 fighters.

JAPANESE SAILORS WAVING OFF THEIR PLANES

7:45 AM — Dive-bombers attacked local airfields to give the Japanese control of the air. In all, 188 US planes were destroyed.

7:53 AM — The Japanese aimed bombs and torpedoes at the 8 battleships anchored in the harbor.

8:10 AM — The USS *Arizona* was hit by a bomb that ignited the gunpowder in its hold (cargo deck). In the ensuing explosion, 1,177 men died.

8:54 AM — A second wave of 78 dive-bombers, 54 bombers, and 35 fighters arrived to attack the other 76 ships in the harbor, plus oil tanks and docks.

9:55 AM — The second-wave planes returned to their carriers. They left behind 19 badly damaged or sunk ships— and a shocked nation. Comparatively few Japanese planes—29—were lost in the attack.

2,403

Americans were killed in the attack on Pearl Harbor

Culture during wartime

Both at home and on the front line, wartime music, radio shows, and movies expressed what people were fighting for and how much they missed their loved ones. People could escape their troubles for a while when they listened to a comedy on the radio or danced to the latest popular songs. Media had a more serious side, too, as governments everywhere used it to persuade citizens that their cause was right.

Hollywood's leading role

Eager to forget the hardships of war, people flocked to movie theaters to watch musicals and comedies. Hollywood helped the US government by producing films in which heroes fought evil invaders; the villains were nearly always German, Italian, or Japanese. Female characters in films were often shown doing their part as nurses or spies.

Screen support
Like many movies of the time, *Casablanca* (1942) depicts Nazis as arrogant and members of the resistance as brave. It portrays the US as a haven for the oppressed.

Persuasion
Governments used propaganda (see page 17) at home to explain the war and encourage support for it. They also created propaganda to use against their enemies. Both sides tried to destroy their opponents' morale with radio broadcasts for enemy troops. An Allied tactic was to drop propaganda leaflets into occupied territory.

ENCOURAGING PEOPLE TO WORK AND FIGHT

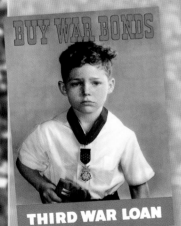

RAISING MONEY FOR THE WAR EFFORT

BUILDING A SENSE OF NATIONAL IDENTITY

SHOWING THE ENEMY AS EVIL

[Winning minds]

Super sounds
"Big band" groups performed jazz and swing on the radio and in dance halls. Pianist Duke Ellington's band was one of the most popular.

All that jazz
Radio was how most people heard music, and it helped popularize jazz and swing. Hitler tried to ban jazz because of its links with African Americans and Jews, but many German troops listened to it.

Boosting morale
The United Service Organizations (USO) put on up to 700 shows a day to keep up the spirits of US servicemen and women around the world. Stars of USO "camp shows" ranged from Laurel and Hardy to Lucille Ball. German troops had "front theater" plays and cabarets.

Zarah Leander
Deep-voiced Swedish singer Zarah Leander was a superstar in Germany. She fled the country after her home was bombed in 1944.

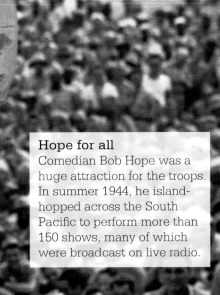

Hope for all
Comedian Bob Hope was a huge attraction for the troops. In summer 1944, he island-hopped across the South Pacific to perform more than 150 shows, many of which were broadcast on live radio.

More here
For key to symbols, see page 112

swing music jazz **jive**
USO **ENSA** "Lili Marlene"
Glenn Miller propaganda

Propaganda
by Charlie Samuels

The Art of War: The Posters of World War II
by Sean Price

The Great Dictator (1940), starring Charlie Chaplin, lampoons Hitler and his treatment of Jews.

Frank Capra's **Why We Fight** (1942–45) is a series of US propaganda films.

Disney's *Der Fuehrer's Face* (1942) features Donald Duck as a factory worker in Nazi Germany.

49th Parallel (1941) is about stranded U-boat sailors in Canada, trying to reach the still-neutral US.

Mrs. Miniver (1942) shows the effect of the war on a British housewife.

"We're Going to Hang Out the Washing on the Siegfried Line" is a comic British song about the German defensive line.

"Rosie the Riveter" is about a female assembly-line worker, who later also appeared on posters.

"When the Atom Bomb Fell" shows US attitudes at the end of the war.

"GI Jive," by Johnny Mercer, was a hit jive song.

Women and the war

These assembly-line workers are completing a B-17 bomber. During the war, the United States' female workforce rose from 12 to 18 million; there were similar increases in other fighting countries. Women took on everything from working on farms and driving buses and trains to operating radar, spying, and, of course, fighting. From 1945, millions of *Trümmerfrauen* ("rubble women") cleared Germany's wrecked cities brick by brick.

Wartime childhood [Tough

War destroyed childhoods, as youngsters dealt with the losses of fathers, mothers, and homes. Everywhere, children struggled with shortages of food, clothes, and toys. Millions fled from battle zones or occupying armies. And millions more were killed by terrible bombings and in the Holocaust (see pages 42–45).

Germany

In Germany, children aged 10–18 were expected to join Nazi youth organizations. Girls cared for the wounded in hospitals. Boys in the Hitler Youth were trained to help during air raids. They operated searchlights, fired antiaircraft guns, and participated in the cleanup.

Eyewitness

NAME: Emmy Werner

DATE: Born in 1929

FROM: Near Frankfurt, Germany

DETAILS: Emmy Werner was 10 when her country went to war. She later moved to the United States and became a psychologist.

❝ I was 12 . . . and volunteered for the . . . air-raid watch. . . . We became experts at spotting incendiaries that had penetrated the roof of our schoolhouse or the classroom ceilings. Armed with buckets, we would race to throw sand over the eight-sided metal sticks before they exploded. ❞

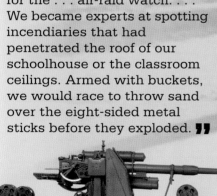

Antiaircraft gun
From January 1943, boys in the Hitler Youth worked German antiaircraft guns.

Eyewitness

NAME: Shizue Kobayashi

DATE: Born in 1934

FROM: Saitama-ken, Japan

DETAILS: Shizue Kobayashi lived in Japan until she was 22 years old. In 1956, she immigrated to the United States to marry an airman who used to play baseball with the children at an orphanage she visited.

❝ I wasn't allowed to eat as much as I wanted, just enough to keep me alive. After our potatoes were gone, we ate weeds we found in the yard. We were lucky, though, because a lot of people were dying of hunger. ❞

Japan

Bombings and food shortages forced many Japanese families to move from the cities to the countryside. The most nimble-fingered girls worked in factories, making fire balloons—bomb-carrying hydrogen balloons that were launched toward the United States and Canada.

times]

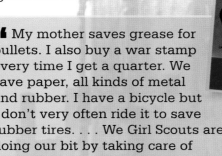

United States

American children helped the war effort by collecting newspapers, rubber tires, and tin cans for recycling. In the month of October 1942, 30 million children collected 1.5 million tons of scrap metal for producing aircraft and munitions.

Eyewitness

NAME: Joan Dooley

DATE: 1942

FROM: Wichita, KS

DETAILS: Joan Dooley was a 12-year-old Girl Scout when she wrote to General Douglas MacArthur, supreme commander of the southwest Pacific war.

❝ My mother saves grease for bullets. I also buy a war stamp every time I get a quarter. We save paper, all kinds of metal and rubber. I have a bicycle but I don't very often ride it to save rubber tires. . . . We Girl Scouts are doing our bit by taking care of small children so that the parents may work in war factories.❞

War bonds
Even children were encouraged to buy war bonds, which raised money for the war effort.

Britain

In Britain, hundreds of thousands of children were evacuated from bomb-threatened cities to the safer but unfamiliar countryside. Candy was rationed, along with other foods, and any treats were highly prized. Children swapped old toys and books and wished for new, war-themed books about tanks, battleships, or warplanes.

Eyewitness

NAME: Jean Bruce

DATE: Born in 1935

FROM: Manchester, Britain

DETAILS: Jean Bruce was 3 years old when the war started, but she remembers the air raids, rationing, and her Mickey Mouse gas mask. She later immigrated to Canada.

❝ People had to queue up for everything (though rationing made things fairer). Sometimes Mum would see a queue forming and join it, not even knowing what was for sale at that shop. One orange was a very rare treat carefully shared out segment by segment, and I didn't have a banana throughout the war. ❞

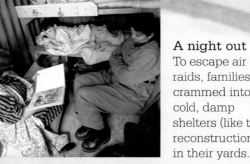

Ruined Berlin
For children in cities across Europe, the daily walk to school became a trek across a bomb site.

A night out
To escape air raids, families crammed into cold, damp shelters (like this reconstruction) in their yards.

More here

For key to symbols, see page 112

Remember World War II: Kids Who Survived Tell Their Stories by Dorinda Makanaonalani Nicholson

Rosie the Riveter: Women in World War II by Sean Stewart Price

The Machine Gunners by Robert Westall

Goodnight Mister Tom (1999) and ***Carrie's War*** (2006) are both adapted from books about evacuated children.

Look out for reruns or the DVDs of ***Hogan's Heroes***, a comedy series about POWs in wartime Germany.

"Any Bonds Today?," sung by the singing trio the Andrews Sisters, encouraged people to help fund the war by buying government war bonds.

"We'll Meet Again," by the English performer Vera Lynn, was a sentimental song about soldiers leaving behind their families.

Experience the sights, sounds, and smells of the Blitz, and step inside an air-raid shelter in the Second World War Galleries at the **Imperial War Museum London**, UK.

Explore the home front gallery and theater at the **Wright Museum of WWII History**, in Wolfeboro, NH.

Sea battles [Pacific turning

By early 1942, Japan was victorious throughout the Pacific and Southeast Asia, so it needed to defend the supply routes to these conquests against attacks by the Allied fleet. The Pacific became a war zone, where submarines, warships, and aircraft carriers battled.

MAP KEY
- Japanese territory
- Allied territory

Battle of Midway

Extent of Japanese control, July 1942

Battle of the Coral Sea

MANCHURIA
JAPAN
CHINA
BURMA
PHILIPPINES
THAILAND
NEW GUINEA
AUSTRALIA

Battle of the Coral Sea: losses

	US	Japan
Aircraft carriers	1	1
Warships	1	4
Oil tankers	1	0
Aircraft	66	77
Men	654	1,074

Battle of the Coral Sea

In May 1942, Japan and the US engaged in a battle in the Coral Sea. The ships involved never saw or fired on one another. Instead, each side used an aircraft carrier to launch bombers to attack the enemy fleet. After four days, the result was a costly draw.

Reasons for war

The Battles of the Coral Sea and Midway were both fought to keep Japan from capturing more bases in the Pacific.

Battle of Midway

Japan planned to draw out the US fleet with a decoy attack on the Aleutian Islands. On June 4, 1942, one force would ambush the US carriers off Midway Island while another conquered Midway itself. However, the US had cracked Japan's coded messages. It hit the Japanese with waves of torpedoes and dive-bombers. Midway was a turning point in the Pacific war. Japan never recovered from its losses.

Battle of Midway: losses		
	US	Japan
Aircraft carriers	1	4
Warships	1	1
Aircraft	132	275
Men	307	3,507

Doomed aircraft carrier

Allied planes were launched from USS *Yorktown*. The carrier was damaged at Coral Sea and sunk just after the Battle of Midway.

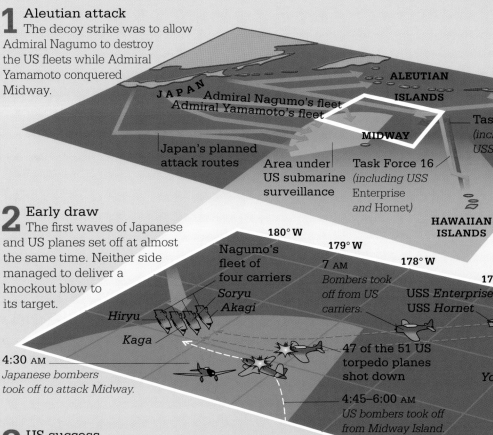

1 Aleutian attack
The decoy strike was to allow Admiral Nagumo to destroy the US fleets while Admiral Yamamoto conquered Midway.

JAPAN
ALEUTIAN ISLANDS
Admiral Nagumo's fleet
Admiral Yamamoto's fleet
MIDWAY
Task Force 17 *(including USS* Yorktown*)*
Japan's planned attack routes
Area under US submarine surveillance
Task Force 16 *(including USS* Enterprise *and* Hornet*)*
HAWAIIAN ISLANDS

2 Early draw
The first waves of Japanese and US planes set off at almost the same time. Neither side managed to deliver a knockout blow to its target.

180° W
179° W
178° W
177° W
Nagumo's fleet of four carriers
Soryu
Akagi
Hiryu
Kaga
7 AM
Bombers took off from US carriers.
USS *Enterprise*
USS *Hornet*
4:30 AM
Japanese bombers took off to attack Midway.
47 of the 51 US torpedo planes shot down
USS *Yorktown*
4:45–6:00 AM
US bombers took off from Midway Island.
30° N

3 US success
While the Japanese fought off one wave of US attackers, another US group got through and hit three carriers.

Hit
Akagi, Soryu, and Kaga sank.
12 PM
USS Yorktown *was hit.*
11 AM
Dive-bombers were launched from Hiryu.
8:30 AM
All three US carriers launched planes to attack Nagumo's fleet.

Backup
Planes from USS Hornet *headed to protect Midway Island.*

4 Massive defeat
Hiryu launched planes at USS *Yorktown* before it sank. Admiral Yamamoto's approaching fleet had to retreat.

June 5
Hiryu sank.
5:05 PM
Hiryu was severely hit.
1:30 PM
Torpedo bombers were launched from Hiryu.
3:30 PM
USS Enterprise launched dive-bombers to attack Hiryu.
2:40 PM
USS Yorktown *was badly hit.*

MAP KEY
■ US Task Force 17
US Task Force 16
Japanese fleets

Jungle fighting [Bullets and

From December 1941, Japan invaded many Pacific islands, as well as Asian countries such as Malaya and Burma. It quickly learned how to fight in the dense jungle. Now US, British, Australian, and other Allied troops had to do the same. This fighting was up close and nasty, as small groups crawled on their bellies or waded through swamps.

Under attack

Enemies could be lurking above- or belowground—but they were only one of the dangers soldiers faced in the jungle. Troops on both sides feared mosquito bites, which could transmit deadly malaria or dengue fever.

Jungle worries
For every 1 combat casualty, Allied doctors treated as many as 100 soldiers suffering from heatstroke or tropical diseases.

Extreme heat
Temperatures could soar to 100°F (38°C), causing exhaustion and dehydration.

Malaria
This disease caused fever, convulsions, and death.

Tall grass
Razor-sharp kunai grass cut through flesh like a knife.

Leeches
These bloodsuckers left wounds that could soon become infected.

Bad water
Microorganisms in dirty water led to dysentery, cholera, and typhoid.

Venomous snakes
Vipers could kill with a single bite.

Dengue fever
This virus led to fever, rashes, and even death.

Jungle rot
Tropical ulcers formed on the skin and rotted away the flesh.

Eyewitness

NAME: George Henry Johnston

DATE: 1942

FROM: Melbourne, Australia

DETAILS: Johnston (1912–70) was a war correspondent for the *Melbourne Argus* newspaper.

❝ Churned up by the troops of both armies, the track itself is now knee-deep in thick black mud. For the last ten days no man's clothing has been dry, and all have slept when sleep was possible in pouring rain under sodden blankets. Each man carries his personal equipment, firearms, ammunition supply, and five days' rations. Every hour is a nightmare. ❞

Mud march
In November 1943, US marines headed to Bougainville Island, part of New Guinea, to confront the Japanese.

80%
of US soldiers in some South Pacific units were infected with malaria

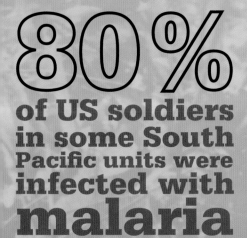

Japanese tactics

Japanese snipers lashed themselves to trees or hid in dugouts in order to surprise the enemy, particularly at night. They would call out in English to trick Allies in the dark, and they always fought to the death.

Dugout
The main bunker could house a small detachment of troops.

Crawl trench
These tunnels connected the dugout to the foxholes.

Foxhole
One-man gun pits radiated out from the main dugout.

Dugout walls
Bamboo or corrugated iron strengthened the walls.

Fire!
The sniper or machine gunner fired through a slit in the wall.

Hideout
Both sides used dugouts like this one to rest in between patrols or as bases for surprise sniper attacks.

Camouflage
Earth, brushwood, or leaves hid the whole complex from sight.

Holdouts

Japanese troops were trained not to give up. Some, left behind in remote areas, never heard that the war was over. These soldiers stayed in their jungle dugouts for years, or even decades, because no one had ordered them to leave.

Holdout Hiroo Onoda surrenders
Officer Hiroo Onoda was 52 when he handed over his sword, dagger, rifle, and hand grenades in 1974. He had hidden in the Philippines for nearly 30 years.

POWs [Incarcerated]

All sides held POWs, or prisoners of war—captured soldiers, airmen, and sailors—in camps to prevent them from fighting again. In countries that had signed the Geneva Conventions, such as Britain and the United States, POWs were mostly treated well. In the Soviet Union and Japan, they were starved and beaten.

International parcels
Some fortunate POWs received Red Cross packages containing treats such as butter, cookies, chocolate, and dried food.

Camps in the West
POW camps were set up all over Europe and the United States. Prisoners occupied themselves with craftwork, reading, and learning new skills. Sometimes they worked on local farms or built roads and waterways. For most, it was a boring but safe wait for the war to end.

Field work
POWs in Britain could not escape their island prison, and many were trusted to work on farms.

Eyewitness
NAME: Janina Skrzynska
POW: Dec. 1944–Apr. 1945
FROM: Poland
DETAILS: Skrzynska was in the Polish Home Army; she was captured by the Nazis after the Warsaw Uprising. She was held in a women's camp at Oberlangen, Germany.

❝ One barrack was used as a chapel, while two more were left empty. These we exploited as an extra supply of fuel: We took out planks from the bunks, pulled up floorboards. . . . In the mornings and evenings [we had] a tepid herbal tea, . . . moldy bread, the occasional piece of margarine, or a spoonful of beetroot marmalade. At midday, . . . soup from bitter cabbage or grubby peas with two or three jacket potatoes. ❞

Colditz Castle
This fortress near Dresden, Germany, was for POWs whose escapes had failed. The war ended before they could fly the glider they had built in the attic!

Great escapes
Allied POWs in Germany made many escape attempts. Their efforts ranged from making fake guard uniforms and simply walking out, to digging tunnels to get beyond the fences. Of the 76 who tried this one night from Stalag Luft III, 3 made it back to Britain, 23 were returned to the camp, and 50 were shot on Hitler's orders.

Camps in the East

Life for prisoners in Japanese POW camps was extremely harsh. POWs were fed tiny amounts of rice. Beatings were common, and POWs were forced to work in mines or on a railroad between Burma and Thailand.

March of death
In April 1942, the Japanese marched captured soldiers 85 miles (135 km) in six days to a camp. They beat or killed those who fell—10,000 Filipinos and 650 Americans died.

Eyewitness

NAME: Thomas Arthur Craigg, Jr.

DATE: Born January 20, 1918

POW: May 6, 1942–Aug. 26, 1945

FROM: Arkansas

DETAILS: Gunnery Sergeant Craigg was wounded in action on May 2, 1942, at Corregidor, while defending the Philippines. He was taken prisoner by the Japanese and transported in a "hell ship" to Japan, where he was forced to work in coal mines 12 hours a day.

❝ We was on one ration a day of rice. That ration of rice didn't amount to much more than a coffee cup full of rice. But that's what we had to eat for sometime. And it wasn't long until things begin to taper off a little bit, not so many people dying. The stronger had survived and we was put on working details, whatever the Japanese had for us to do. Some of us went out to help repair bridges. Some details left and went back to the air force field that we had there and do repair work on that. And others would go and do repair work on bridges, on roads. ❞

60,000
Allied POWs were forced to help build the Burma Railway; one in five died

Changi prisoners
Changi was a notoriously tough Japanese POW camp in Singapore, where inmates had a simple choice—work or starve.

More here

For key to symbols, see page 112

Prisoner of War
by Stewart Ross

Life as a POW
by John F. Wukovits

The Great Escape (1963) is an exciting film based on true stories of Allied POW escapes.

The Colditz Story (1955) is about the many attempted escapes from this fortress.

The **Aliceville POW Museum**, in Aliceville, AL, has artwork and objects made by German POWs.

Geneva Conventions: a series of articles that describe how injured soldiers and POWs should be treated. The first convention was introduced in 1864; Japan and the Soviet Union did not sign the 1929 convention.

hell ship: a Japanese ship carrying Allied POWs crammed into the holds, with little to eat or drink.

Polish Home Army: a resistance movement in Poland that fought against Nazi and Soviet occupation.

Red Cross: an international organization founded in Switzerland in 1863 to help victims of conflict. It sent 36 million aid parcels during the war.

stalag: a German POW camp. The largest, Stalag VII-A, held 130,000 Allied soldiers.

B-24 [Long-range bomber]

More B-24 Liberators were built than any other US military plane. This long-range bomber flew faster and farther than other planes, and with heavier loads. But it burned quickly if its fuel tanks were hit, so it was nicknamed the "flying coffin."

18 hours: the time taken to build each B-24 Liberator

Building B-24s
Ford's Willow Run plant, near Detroit, MI, was built for making B-24s. The assembly line was 1 mile (1.6 km) long.

Oxygen bottles
Spare oxygen was for the crew to breathe.

All-arounder
The B-24 was far more than just a heavy bomber. It could attack submarines and ships, lay mines, transport people and supplies, and carry out photographic reconnaissance missions and weather checks.

Top gun turret
The plane's engineer manned the gun in this Plexiglas turret.

Cockpit crew
B-24 pilots needed strength to handle the heavy controls.

Nose turret
This protective turret had a shield of bulletproof Plexiglas.

Machine guns
These .50-caliber guns could fire 800 rounds a minute.

Electric heaters
Heaters kept the guns from freezing in the cold, high air.

Nose wheel
This prevented the plane from tipping when on the ground.

Bomb bay doors
The doors rolled back into the fuselage to keep the plane streamlined.

Bombs away!
Most B-24s carried ten 500 lb. (227 kg) bombs, or five 1,000 lb. (454 kg) ones.

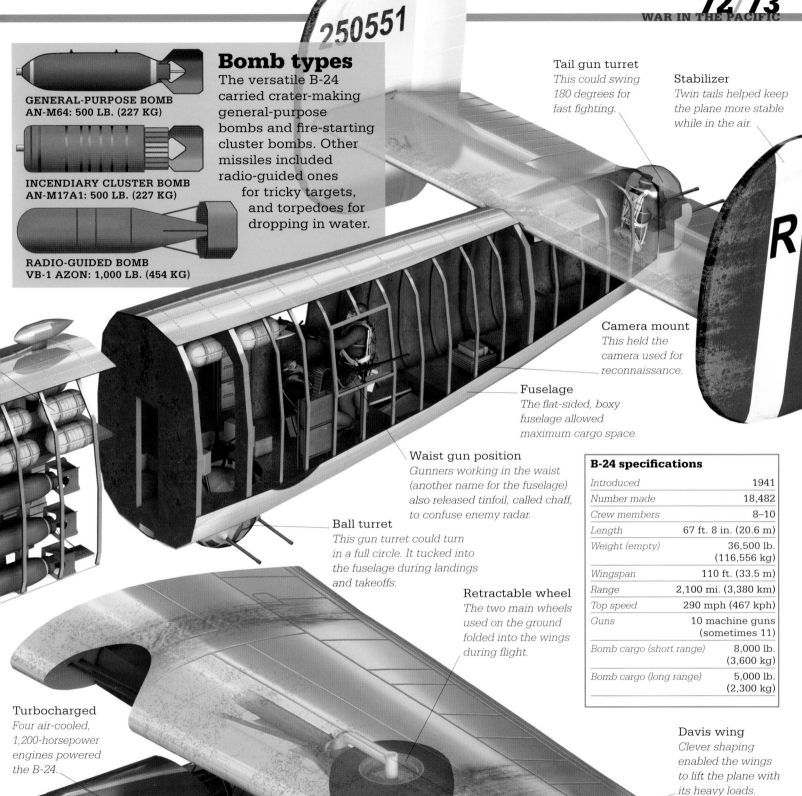

250551

Bomb types

The versatile B-24 carried crater-making general-purpose bombs and fire-starting cluster bombs. Other missiles included radio-guided ones for tricky targets, and torpedoes for dropping in water.

**GENERAL-PURPOSE BOMB
AN-M64: 500 LB. (227 KG)**

**INCENDIARY CLUSTER BOMB
AN-M17A1: 500 LB. (227 KG)**

**RADIO-GUIDED BOMB
VB-1 AZON: 1,000 LB. (454 KG)**

Tail gun turret
This could swing 180 degrees for fast fighting.

Stabilizer
Twin tails helped keep the plane more stable while in the air.

Camera mount
This held the camera used for reconnaissance.

Fuselage
The flat-sided, boxy fuselage allowed maximum cargo space.

Waist gun position
Gunners working in the waist (another name for the fuselage) also released tinfoil, called chaff, to confuse enemy radar.

Ball turret
This gun turret could turn in a full circle. It tucked into the fuselage during landings and takeoffs.

Retractable wheel
The two main wheels used on the ground folded into the wings during flight.

Turbocharged
Four air-cooled, 1,200-horsepower engines powered the B-24.

Davis wing
Clever shaping enabled the wings to lift the plane with its heavy loads.

B-24 specifications

Introduced	1941
Number made	18,482
Crew members	8–10
Length	67 ft. 8 in. (20.6 m)
Weight (empty)	36,500 lb. (116,556 kg)
Wingspan	110 ft. (33.5 m)
Range	2,100 mi. (3,380 km)
Top speed	290 mph (467 kph)
Guns	10 machine guns (sometimes 11)
Bomb cargo (short range)	8,000 lb. (3,600 kg)
Bomb cargo (long range)	5,000 lb. (2,300 kg)

Jungle warfare through Southeast Asia was slow and deadly. The Allies needed a different strategy against the Japanese. From June 1943, they began to conquer islands around powerful Japanese bases. As the Allies gained control of sea and air, they were able to keep supplies from reaching enemy troops. This leapfrogging to the next target en route to Japan itself was called island-hopping.

Kamikaze killers

The Japanese adopted a terrifying new tactic in October 1944 at the Battle of Leyte Gulf—kamikaze, or "divine wind," attacks. Pilots flew bomb-filled planes straight into targets. By the end of the war, the Japanese had carried out about 2,800 of these suicide missions.

In for the kill
A kamikaze fighter plane hurtles toward the USS *Missouri*, off Okinawa, in April 1945. The battleship survived the attack.

MANCHURIA

KOREA

Sea of Japan

JAPAN

East China Sea

Okinawa
June 1945

CHINA

BURMA

South China Sea

PHILIPPINES

4 End of the line
The advancing Allied lines met at Okinawa, which became their base for air attacks on Japan.

Iwo Jima
Feb.–Mar. 1945

3 Leyte Gulf
In October 1944, Japan counterattacked in the Battle of Leyte Gulf. Much of its fleet was destroyed.

Philippine Sea
June 1944

Leyte Gulf
Oct. 1944

PALAU ISLANDS

Mindanao

Peleliu
Sept.–Nov. 1944

Morotai
Sept. 1944

DUTCH BORNEO

Banda Sea

NEW GUINEA

JAVA

Timor Sea

AUSTRALIA

The fleet train

Supplies are vital in any war. To fight in the Pacific, US troops, ships, and aircraft had to be fed, fueled, and armed 5,000 miles (8,000 km) away from the US mainland. The solution was the fleet train, a convoy of tankers and other ships that could replenish supplies at sea.

TYPES OF SHIP IN A CONVOY

DESTROYER

ESCORT CARRIER

CARGO SHIP

TROOP TRANSPORTER

MUNITIONS SHIP

GASOLINE TANKER

OIL TANKER

HOSPITAL SHIP

Attack ships

Destroyers and escort carriers were ready to attack Japanese submarines, ships, or planes that came too close.

Supply ships

Tankers and ships carried massive stocks of the chilled and dried foods, fresh water, fuel, and munitions needed to fight a war.

1.5 million
Japanese servicemen died in the Pacific War, compared to 103,000 US troops

Route of Allied attack fleet, led by Admiral Nimitz from the naval base at Pearl Harbor

Pearl Harbor

HAWAIIAN ISLANDS

Saipan
July 1944

Tinian
July 1944

Guam
July 1944

MARIANA ISLANDS

Enewetak
Feb. 1944

Kwajalein
Feb. 1944

MARSHALL ISLANDS

CHUUK ISLANDS

Japan's major Pacific base

2 Leapfrogging
From 1943, the Allies encircled key Japanese strongholds, such as the massive Chuuk Lagoon base and the southern base at Rabaul.

GILBERT ISLANDS

Admiralty Islands
Feb.–May 1944

Tarawa
Nov. 1943

Rabaul
Japanese base

Bougainville
Nov. 1943

SOLOMON ISLANDS

Guadalcanal
Aug. 1942–Feb. 1943

Route of Allied attack fleet, led by General MacArthur from the naval base at Brisbane, Australia

Pacific progress

The Allies' ultimate target was the Japanese mainland. In 1942, a series of sea battles, especially the Battle of Midway (see page 65), weakened Japan's navy and air force. Then, in June 1943, Operation Cartwheel began—the island-hopping strategy to isolate Japan's Pacific bases.

MAP KEY
- - - Extent of Japanese control, July 1942
■ Japanese territory
□ Allied territory
✳ Allied victory

1 Two lines of attack
There were two prongs to the fight. One went across the central Pacific (blue line), the other across the southwest Pacific (yellow line).

The Battle of Iwo Jima

Iwo Jima is a tiny Pacific island 700 miles (1,100 km) from Japan's capital, Tokyo. Allied planes needed to use its airstrips for attacks on the Japanese mainland. It was a key target.

As many as 21,000 Japanese defenders on Iwo Jima dug bunkers connected by 11 miles (18 km) of tunnels. On February 19, 1945, they watched 30,000 US marines land on the beaches, then started firing. When the fierce fighting ended five weeks later, only 212 Japanese remained alive. Japan's unshakable willingness to fight to the end led the United States toward its decision to drop atomic bombs and end the war.

War in A
& the Mid

* Which German general was known as the Desert Fox?

* What dangers did tank commanders face?

* How did the Allies win their victory at El Alamein?

frica

dle East

Africa and the Middle East

For 32 months, starting from September 1940, Allied and Axis forces battled back and forth in North and East Africa. This was a deadly game of chess played across the hot desert with tanks, artillery, and troops. The prize was access to Middle Eastern oil.

APR. 1941
The siege of Tobruk
Rommel's forces surrounded and bombarded Tobruk, trapping 14,000 Australians. Fighting back from a defensive network of trenches and tunnels, the Australian troops nicknamed themselves "the rats of Tobruk."

GERMAN TROOPS AND TANKS NEAR TOBRUK

JULY 1940
Naval attack
The British wanted to keep the Germans from taking control of the French fleet in the Algerian port of Mers El Kébir. They attacked, sinking three battleships.

BATTLESHIPS ON FIRE AT MERS EL KÉBIR, ALGERIA

JAN. 1941
Allied forces swept on from Egypt to take the key port of Tobruk, in Libya.

DEC. 1941
The Allies forced Rommel's army away from Tobruk to relieve the siege.

1941 **1942**

Dots represent yearly increases.

JUNE 10, 1940
Italy declared war on Britain and France. Mussolini had 300,000 Italian and African troops based in Libya.

JULY 1940
In East Africa, Italy attacked the British colonies of Sudan and Kenya.

DEC. 1940
British troops, numbering 36,000, defeated a force of 75,000 Italians in Egypt.

NOV. 27, 1941
Italian forces lost a key battle at Gondar, Abyssinia (now Ethiopia), with the surrender of 23,500 men. Italy was finally forced out of East Africa.

22,195
gallons (85,000 L): the amount of fuel the Afrika Korps needed every week

ERWIN ROMMEL

German army

In Africa:	Feb. 1941–May 1943
Rank in 1941:	General
Nickname:	The Desert Fox

FEB. 1941
The Afrika Korps
German forces, battle hardened from their successes in Europe, arrived to support the struggling Italians. The German Afrika Korps was led by Rommel, an experienced and clever general.

JULY 1–27, 1942
First Battle of El Alamein

The small Egyptian town was the last line of Allied defense before the Suez Canal. Allies and Germans battled to a draw that weakened Rommel's overextended army.

A BRITISH 5.5-INCH (14 CM) ARTILLERY GUN USED AT EL ALAMEIN

JULY 10, 1943
Invasion of Sicily

It took a total of 450,000 Allied soldiers 38 days to drive retreating Italian and German troops from the island of Sicily in the Mediterranean Sea. For this mission, code-named Operation Husky, Allied troops arrived by boat and by parachute.

BRITISH TROOPS LANDING ON SICILY

NOV. 8–14, 1942
To the east, in Operation Torch, the Allies landed in French North Africa.

JAN. 1943
The British took Tripoli, in Libya, forcing the Axis armies back east into Tunisia.

SEPT. 8, 1943
Italy surrendered. Allied troops had invaded five days earlier, and they kept advancing from the south.

1943   **1944•**

MAY 1942
Rommel's attack at Gazala, Libya, pushed the Allies back into Egypt.

JUNE 21, 1942
The German Afrika Korps captured Tobruk and 35,000 Allied troops.

AUG. 1942
The first of 300 US Sherman tanks arrived in North Africa. They were to prove vital.

FEB. 19–25, 1943
The Battle of Kasserine Pass was Rommel's last victory, as his forces beat the newly arrived US troops.

MAY 1943
With hardly any supplies left, Axis forces surrendered in Tunisia.

OCT. 13, 1943
Italy switched sides and declared war on Germany, its former ally.

AUG. 1942
Troop morale

General Bernard Montgomery took command of the British Eighth Army. He made speeches directly to his troops, explaining how he planned to defeat Rommel. This made him very popular.

BERNARD MONTGOMERY

British army

In Africa: Aug. 1942 – May 1943

Rank in 1942:   General

Nickname: Monty

OCT. 23–NOV. 4, 1942
Second Battle of El Alamein

Montgomery used rubber tanks, wooden trucks, and dummy railroads to deceive the Germans. His victory at El Alamein marked the point at which Rommel began his retreat.

AN INFLATABLE RUBBER DECOY TANK

War in the desert [Sand

War came to North Africa in September 1940, when Italy used its African colony Libya as the base for an advance on British-occupied Egypt. Mussolini's ultimate target was the crucial Suez Canal. When the Allies pushed the Italians back, Hitler sent his Afrika Korps to the fight. Now the desert war raged.

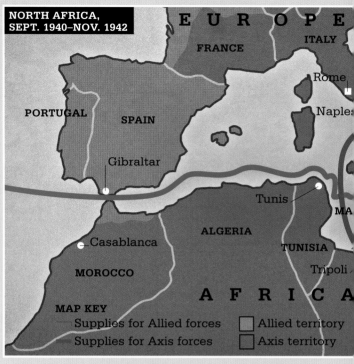

NORTH AFRICA, SEPT. 1940–NOV. 1942

EUROPE
FRANCE
ITALY
Rome
Naples
PORTUGAL
SPAIN
Gibraltar
Tunis
MA
ALGERIA
TUNISIA
Casablanca
Tripoli
MOROCCO
AFRICA

MAP KEY
— Supplies for Allied forces
— Supplies for Axis forces
☐ Allied territory
☐ Axis territory

Combined forces
Thousands of Australians and New Zealanders, known as ANZACs, fought in Africa alongside soldiers from India, South Africa, and all over the British empire. During July 1942 and again in October, they fought the Germans for control of El Alamein, Egypt.

Digging trenches
In August 1942, these New Zealanders dug trenches to defend the patch of desert that they had won at the First Battle of El Alamein.

Supply routes
Resources were scarce in this undeveloped territory, much of which was desert, so both sides had to bring all their supplies. Tobruk was a major prize because it was the port nearest to the front lines, where the armies needed food, fuel, and ammunition in vast quantities.

Into Africa
Allied supplies came along the Suez Canal or through the British territory Gibraltar. Axis supplies sailed into Tripoli, then trucked along the coast road.

Fighting team
Hitler created his Afrika Korps in February 1941, selecting his popular commander Erwin Rommel to lead it. Rommel used the Wehrmacht's fast, surprise blitzkrieg methods (see pages 22–23) brilliantly.

Minefields
Millions of mines were hidden just below the sand, primed to blow up if tanks drove over them.

Moving at night
Troop movements across the open desert took place at night, under cover of darkness.

Desert tactics
Both sides often began attacks with blasts of artillery; then the infantry would advance, supported by tanks. It was important to stay within reach of supplies, or fuel-hungry tanks might be stranded. Spies provided intelligence about where the other side was and where it was going.

Decoy tanks
Tanks dragged metal chains to create clouds of dust that looked like an army on the move.

Poisoning water
If troops retreated, they poisoned water supplies to keep this vital resource from the enemy.

Sun goggles
Goggles blocked the sun and the windblown sand. Rommel had a favorite pair, which he captured from a British officer.

Hard times
Desert conditions were tough. The days were blisteringly hot but the nights were cold. Vehicles and shell fire whipped up sandstorms, and the grit turned the tiniest scratches into painful sores. Food spoiled in the heat, dysentery was common, and water was too scarce to waste on washing.

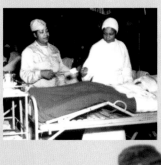

Medical care
Casualties were treated at field hospitals. The use of penicillin and blood transfusions saved millions of lives.

Eyewitness

NAME: Hans Klein

DATE: Born in 1921

FROM: Germany

DETAILS: Klein was a furniture maker before he joined the German forces. He served as a private in the Afrika Korps from 1942 to 1943 and was awarded the Iron Cross medal for bravery.

❝ Flies were a problem, and we had no control over them. Nets that we wore over our faces at all times protected us from the flies and allowed us to enjoy eating. To eat some bread with jelly, first you had to get all the flies off the bread and then quickly slip it under your net—hoping not to bring them all inside the net with you. ❞

Popular leader
Rommel (far left) inspired great respect from his troops. He lived, ate, and fought alongside his men, and cared for their welfare.

The most dangerous wartime missions were behind enemy lines. Spies risked their lives learning about troop movements, weapons development, and other sensitive information. Special forces attacked key targets such as supply lines.

Special ops

All sides had special operations (ops) units. Their operatives were trained in close combat so that they could kill an enemy guard in a prison or munitions factory without the noise of a gun raising an alarm.

Special Air Service

The British SAS was formed in July 1941 to attack behind German lines in North Africa. In one early mission, an SAS force blew up 60 German aircraft without a single British casualty.

Scouts and Raiders

Formed in the US in 1942, the Scouts and Raiders specialized in underwater reconnaissance. Many of their missions involved supporting troop landings.

Spy rings

All countries had intelligence agencies and spies. Many spies worked in counterespionage, or stopping enemy spies. Some were double agents who passed on false information.

US OSS

The Office of Strategic Services was the US's first spy agency; its staff was trained by the British secret services. It ran spy networks around the world and later became the CIA.

Founded:	1942
Operatives:	24,000
Known for:	Spying in Nazi Germany; supporting partisans against Japan

SPY: VIRGINIA HALL

US agent Hall worked in Vichy France for the SOE and then the OSS. She found sites where weapons for resistance fighters could be dropped, helped airmen who had been shot down escape, and reported on German troop movements. She was nicknamed "the Limping Lady" because of her wooden foot, the result of a hunting accident. Hall died in 1982 at age 76.

British SOE

The Special Operations Executive supported resistance movements in Europe and Asia. Its agents were trained in creating disguises, parachuting, weapons usage, unarmed combat, map reading, and radio communications.

Founded:	July 1940
Operatives:	13,000
Known for:	Helping resistance movements; feeding fake information to the Germans

SPY: JOAN PUJOL GARCIA

Spanish-born Garcia persuaded the Germans to take him on as a spy—but only because he wanted to work as a double agent. His sympathies lay with the British. Garcia gave the Germans fake information about D-Day, convincing them that the landings would take place farther up the coast. After the war, Garcia faked his own death and went to live in Venezuela.

German Abwehr

The Abwehr was the Wehrmacht's military intelligence bureau, loyal to Germany, not to Hitler. It was involved in an attempt on Hitler's life in 1944. The SD, a rival intelligence agency, reported to high-ranking Nazi Heinrich Himmler.

Founded:	1921
Operatives:	Number unknown
Known for:	Infiltrating a Dutch underground unit

SPY: ELYESA BAZNA

Bazna worked for the British ambassador in Turkey, but he was really a German spy, with the code name Cicero. Whenever the ambassador took a bath, Bazna opened a safe and photographed secret documents. The British later claimed that Bazna was a double agent. Double cross became triple cross after the war when Bazna realized that the Abwehr had paid him with counterfeit money.

Soviet GRU

Stalin did not trust anyone, so spies from the GRU, the main Soviet intelligence agency, infiltrated both Allied and Axis powers. GRU agents uncovered German battle plans that proved crucial in winning the Battle of Kursk in July 1943.

Founded:	1921
Operatives:	Thousands (exact number unknown)
Known for:	Stealing information on the atomic bomb

SPY: RICHARD SORGE

Sorge was a German Communist who supported the Soviet Union. He worked as a journalist in Germany, where he joined the Nazi Party as part of his cover. He warned Stalin about Hitler's invasion plans in 1941 but was ignored. Sorge ran a spy network in Japan but was discovered by the Japanese and hanged in 1944. He has been called the greatest spy of all time.

Spy kit

Secret agents used a range of equipment, from simple to of the latest technology. Their spy gear had to be easy to carry and conceal, but quick to work.

Garrote
This length of wire, used to strangle victims, could retract into the handle.

Concealed knife
The 5.5 in. (13.5 cm) blade was released by a button on the handle.

Cudgel
The weighted steel ball could be used to club someone on the head.

Multipurpose weapon

The McLaglen Peskett close-combat weapon was three weapons in one: a garrote (strangle wire), a knife, and a cudgel. Just 7 inches (18 cm) long, it was very easy to hide on the body, perhaps strapped to a leg.

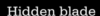

Hidden blade
Blades were hidden in many ways—inside shoe heels, fake coins, or, in this case, an innocent-looking pencil. Blades were useful for cutting tires or wires, as well as people.

Pencil
The wood has been cut away to reveal the blade inside.

Silencer
The silencer muffled the bang of the gun.

Modified Luger

This silenced Luger pistol was part of the kit intended to be used in the attempt to assassinate Hitler on July 20, 1944.

Japanese spies

In Japan, all agents studied the martial art of aikido. Some learned Russian so that they could spy in the Soviet Union. Others scouted Pearl Harbor before the 1941 attack. Many aided local nationalists in Asia, who wanted freedom from western colonial rule.

Founded:	1938
Operatives:	2,500
Known for:	Finding weaknesses in Singapore's defenses

SPY: VELVALEE DICKINSON

US-born Dickinson ran a doll-trading business in New York—but she was also a spy. Writing to an address in Argentina, she sold information to the Japanese. Her letters, intercepted by the FBI, seemed to be about dolls but were in code and actually detailed US naval ship repairs and movements. In 1944, Dickinson was found guilty of espionage and sentenced to ten years in jail.

Sure shot
This tiny camera, about 3.5 in. (9 cm) across, was seized from a spy after the war. Light, small, and easy to conceal, it could take pictures of documents at close range.

Victory in North Africa

The turning point of the war took place in North Africa. In late 1942, General Montgomery led the Allied forces across the desert. The Second Battle of El Alamein shocked Germany into retreat for the first time. Then, as British and US forces poured in, the African coast became the launchpad for an invasion of Italy that brought the battle back into Europe.

African trap
After the Allied triumph at El Alamein, Allied forces stormed ashore in Morocco and Algeria, trapping Rommel in Tunisia. The surrounded Axis forces surrendered on May 13, 1943.

MAP KEY
— Allied fleet
— UK troops
— German troops

Second Battle of El Alamein

SEPT.–OCT. 1942	Rommel laid 3 million mines across the front, in two 5-mile (8 km) belts. To trick Rommel about his tank positions, Montgomery placed dummy tanks to the south and disguised real tanks as trucks.
OCT. 23	After a six-hour artillery barrage, the Allies advanced at night.
OCT. 24	Montgomery's troops slowly cleared paths through the minefields for their advancing columns of tanks.
OCT. 25	To the north, Australian troops captured a key German lookout post, Point 29.
OCT. 26	British bombers sank a German oil tanker in the Mediterranean, off Tobruk, Libya, adding to Rommel's supply problems.
NOV. 2	After a seven-hour artillery barrage, the Allies advanced, punching a 12-mile-wide (19 km) hole in the German lines.
NOV. 3	The advancing Allies found enemy forces ready to surrender or already gone. The Germans left behind thousands of vehicles with empty fuel tanks.
NOV. 9	Rommel's forces lost a key position at Sidi Barrani, in northwestern Egypt.
NOV. 11	Despite Hitler's orders to stand and fight, the Axis forces retreated from Egypt. 25,000 had been killed or wounded, and a further 25,000 had been captured. The Allies suffered just 13,000 casualties.

"The battle is going very heavily against us. We're being crushed by the enemy weight"
—ERWIN ROMMEL, NOVEMBER 3, 1942

5.5 IN. (14 CM) ARTILLERY GUN, BRITISH

The crunch
Fought mostly at night, across a 40-mile-long (64 km) front in the Egyptian desert, the Second Battle of El Alamein halted the Axis advance toward the Middle East and sent the Germans into retreat. Having cracked German codes, the Allies knew that Rommel was ill and short on fuel. His 110,000 troops and 559 tanks were outnumbered by the Allies' 195,000 men and 1,351 tanks, including the new US Shermans.

Monty's men
Montgomery's army combined men from Britain, Australia, India, and New Zealand, as well as Free French forces. Thousands of Germans surrendered to them in Egypt.

Sicily and beyond

The Allies gathered a huge invasion force to cross the Mediterranean, and they began by attacking the island of Sicily. The Germans were not prepared, because they had found a planted body, floating in the sea off Spain, that carried plans of fake invasions. Sicily was captured in August 1943. The Allies invaded Italy on September 3, and Italy surrendered five days later. Germany fought on.

Over the waves
At dawn on July 10, 1943, a fleet of 2,590 ships transported 180,000 troops to the eastern and southwestern coasts of Sicily. In all, 450,000 Allied troops landed during the 38-day battle.

60,000:

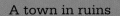

the number of casualties suffered by **both sides at Monte Cassino**

Battle of Monte Cassino

Occupied by German forces, the historic hilltop monastery of Monte Cassino, Italy, blocked the Allies' route north from southern Italy to Rome. The Allies attacked on January 17, 1944, but German troops were able to hold out until May 18.

A town in ruins
Intensive bombing and shelling wrecked Monte Cassino and the town below. Craters and rubble made perfect foxholes for the German defenders.

The
of th

* On which famous day did the Allies invade France?

* What happened after Germany surrendered?

* How did one Little Boy flatten a whole city?

end

e war

D-Day

At dawn on June 6, 1944, Allied troops landed in France to start the attack on Hitler's armies across Europe. This was the scene on Omaha Beach, one of five landing points along a 50-mile (80 km) stretch of the Normandy coast. More than 158,000 men landed on D-Day itself, the first of a total invasion force of 2 million.

More here

For key to symbols, see page 112

D-Day Omaha Beach
Dwight Eisenhower
Utah Beach

D-Day Landings: The Story of the Allied Invasion by Richard Platt

Remember D-Day: The Plan, the Invasion, Survivor Stories by Ronald J. Drez

D-Day Remembered is a documentary about the Normandy landings, with eyewitness accounts.

Ike: Countdown to D-Day focuses on the planning of the invasion by General Dwight Eisenhower.

Visit the **landing beaches** along the Normandy coastline. There are **D-Day museums** in Ouistreham and Arromanches, France.

The **D-Day Museum** in Portsmouth, UK, includes the Overlord Embroidery, a tapestry tribute to the troops involved in D-Day.

D-Day: a military term short for *day day*—the chosen day for a particular event. Specifically, *D-Day* now refers to June 6, 1944.

Battle of the Bulge [Nazi

At the end of 1944, the Allied advance eastward across Europe toward Berlin seemed inevitable. Then, in December, the Germans launched a surprise attack that became known as the Battle of the Bulge. This offensive held up the advance for two months.

Still operational
The Allies destroyed the massive bunkers that were the secret launch sites for Germany's V-2 rockets. But the Nazis continued to launch V-2s from mobile units.

Deadly rockets
Through the winter of 1944–45, around 2,500 people in London alone were killed by V-2s, many of which were launched from country roads in northern Europe.

Stretched thin
The Allies' advance across war-ravaged Europe was filled with difficulties and terrors. The Germans had left mines and booby traps. Snipers hid in ruined buildings. The Allied commanders stretched their lines thin— the 80-mile (130 km) front in the Ardennes, between Belgium and France, was held by 60,000 US troops. When the Germans attacked, they did so with 200,000 men.

Slow progress
Soldiers had to use mine detectors to clear buildings that the retreating Germans had booby-trapped.

Icy warfare
Allied soldiers were forced to fight against almost overwhelming odds in the thick forests and narrow valleys of the Ardennes, in grueling weather. Here, a US Seventh Armored Division patrols the Belgian village of Saint Vith.

Into battle

Hitler wanted to split the British, Canadian, and US armies in the Ardennes, and block a key supply route. The US forces were pushed back, but Allied counterattacks and German fuel shortages ended the battle after six weeks.

The "bulge"

This map shows the bulge created by the advance of 200,000 German soldiers. They found a weak point in the Allied lines.

6 January 25
Weeks of counterattacks forced the Germans to halt the assault.

5 December 23
Better weather allowed Allied planes to fly 15,000 trips in 4 days to attack troops and supply lines.

4 December 21
German troops surrounded and besieged Bastogne, trapping 18,000 US troops.

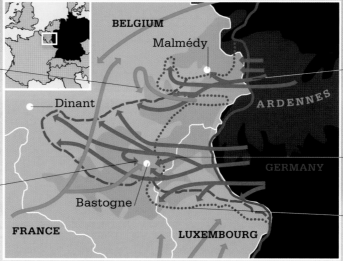

BELGIUM

Malmédy

Dinant

ARDENNES

GERMANY

Bastogne

FRANCE

LUXEMBOURG

1 December 16
The Germans bombarded the Allies. Bad weather prevented a response.

2 December 17
German forces pushed both north and south.

3 December 19
The Germans had now created a bulge in the Allied lines.

Battle of the Bulge: losses	Allied	German
Dead	20,876	15,652
Casualties	42,893	41,600
Captured or missing	23,554	27,582

MAP KEY

—— Allied troops	—— front line Dec. 16
—— German troops	···· front line Dec. 20
Allied territory	– – front line Dec. 25
■ German territory	

Eyewitness

NAME: Robert C. Cable

DATE: 1944

LOCATION: Belgium

DETAILS: From Cleveland, OH, Cable was a 19-year-old soldier in the US Army's Seventeenth Airborne Division. He described the Battle of the Bulge as "the worst Christmas I ever spent."

"

❝The weather conditions were atrocious. We were losing 2,000 men a day, not to combat so much as to the weather. I mean frozen feet, frozen fingers, everything. We had a lot of problems with that.**❞**

Berlin falls [Victory in Europe]

In 1945, as Allied forces advanced on Berlin from east and west, Hitler stayed in his bunker. Stalin was determined to crush the German capital, so the other Allies held back as 2.5 million Red Army troops entered the city. The war in Europe was over, but in the Pacific and Asia, it continued for three more months.

Fall of Berlin

The Russians encircled Berlin and then captured it street by street. Out for revenge, they looted shops and robbed civilians. After Hitler's suicide, German generals eventually had no choice but to surrender.

Soviet advance
On April 30, 1945, Red Army tanks rumbled toward the Reichstag, the German parliamentary building.

Eyewitness

NAME: Dorothea von Schwanenfluegel
DATE: April 20, 1945
DETAILS: Polish-born Schwanenfluegel moved to Germany as a child. In 1945, she was a 29-year-old mother in Berlin.

❝ We noticed a sad-looking young boy across the street, standing behind some bushes in a self-dug, shallow trench. I went over to him and found a mere child in a uniform many sizes too large for him, with an antitank grenade lying beside him. Tears were running down his face, and he was obviously very frightened. . . . [H]e had been ordered to lie in wait here, and when a Soviet tank approached, he was to run under it and explode the grenade. ❞

Fall of Berlin: Time line

Apr. 16 *The Soviets began to bombard Berlin's outer defenses. German deserters were hanged from the trees.*

Apr. 20 *Hitler celebrated his birthday by decorating Hitler Youth boys with medals. The last Anglo-US air raid on Berlin took place.*

Apr. 26 *The Soviets had control of the suburbs. Marshals Zhukov and Konev were competing to claim Berlin.*

Apr. 30 *The battle for the Reichstag began. Hitler and his wife committed suicide. Joseph Goebbels was made chancellor.*

Tea for victory
At this celebratory tea party in London, children ate sandwiches and cake at a giant V-shaped table.

Victory and defeat

War-weary civilians and troops from Allied countries celebrated Victory in Europe (V-E) Day with street parties and dancing. But in German and Italian cities, people starved, as did many others in war-torn lands. Across Europe, 12 million refugees began the long journey home.

Eyewitness

NAME: Mollie Panter-Downes

DATE: May 19, 1945

DETAILS: Born in August 1906, Panter-Downes was an English novelist who wrote the Letter from London column for the *New Yorker* magazine.

❝ The government decided against sounding the sirens in a triumphant 'all clear,' for fear that the noise would revive too many painful memories. For the same reason, there were no salutes of guns—only the pealing of the bells, and the whistles of tugs on the Thames sounding the doot, doot, doot, dooooot of the 'V,' and the roar of the planes, which swooped back and forth over the city, dropping red and green signals toward the blur of smiling, upturned faces. ❞

US celebrations
Jubilant crowds gathered in cities across the US, especially New York. They marked V-E Day with ticker-tape parades, cheering, singing, and triumphant flag-waving.

May 1 *Goebbels and his wife committed suicide after poisoning their six children. Admiral Dönitz became head of Germany.*

May 2 *General Weidling, in charge of Berlin's defenses, surrendered the city on the radio, saying: "Anyone who falls for Berlin dies in vain."*

May 4–5 *Thousands of German troops marched west to surrender to British and US forces rather than to the Soviets.*

May 8 *V-E Day: The Germans officially signed their surrender in Berlin, with Soviet, US, British, and French witnesses.*

Hiroshima

The Pacific war dragged on, and in the summer of 1945, the United States decided to force Japan to surrender by deploying a devastating new weapon: the atomic bomb. Its first target was the city of Hiroshima. When the Japanese did not surrender right away, a second bomb was dropped, on the city of Nagasaki. These powerful weapons produced blistering heat that killed instantly, and deadly radiation that caused death and suffering for years afterward.

AUG. 6

THE ATOMIC BOMB LITTLE BOY

2:45 AM The B-29 bomber *Enola Gay* took off from the Pacific island of Tinian. Its deadly cargo was "Little Boy," the atomic bomb destined for Hiroshima.

8:15 AM Little Boy was dropped on Hiroshima, a city of 300,000 people. A fireball 2,000 feet (600 m) in diameter engulfed everything. At least 70,000 people died instantly.

8:25 AM The mushroom cloud billowed up to a height of 40,000 feet (12,190 m).

AUG. 9 The atomic bomb "Fat Man" was detonated over Nagasaki. The blast killed at least 40,000 people.

AUG. 15 Emperor Hirohito announced on the radio that Japan would surrender.

SEPT. 6 After a month, 70,000 more citizens of Hiroshima had died from burns or radiation sickness.

"The enemy has begun to employ a new, most cruel bomb"
—EMPEROR HIROHITO'S SURRENDER SPEECH

The war in numbers

World War II was the biggest and most terrible war the world has ever seen. There were 61 countries involved, and 1.9 billion of their populations took up arms and fought. About 1 in every 40 people in the world died, many of them civilians. The war lasted so long because Germany and Japan stubbornly fought on even when it was clear that they could not win.

WWII in context

When US president Woodrow Wilson took the United States into World War I in 1917, he called it "a war to end all wars." These casualty statistics show that, sadly, he was wrong.

Different styles

Previous wars were fought by armies charging at one another and fighting hand to hand. World War II was far more destructive.

WORLD WAR II
1939–1945
69,700,000

WORLD WAR I
1914–1918
15,000,000

RUSSIAN CIVIL WAR
1917–1922
9,000,000

THIRTY YEARS' WAR
1618–1648
7,000,000

NAPOLEONIC WARS
1799–1815
4,000,000

CHINESE CIVIL WAR
1927–1950
3,000,000

ENGLISH CIVIL WAR
1642–1651
868,000

AMERICAN CIVIL WAR
1861–1865
620,000

SPANISH CIVIL WAR
1936–1939
500,000

KEY
= 1 million dead

2,174 days

World War II lasted

War machine

The fighting on land, at sea, and in the air called for the production of enormous amounts of extra equipment. Factories in the United States supplied much of the Allied armory. They employed mass-production techniques and recruited 3 million women to work in special war factories, which tremendously boosted the workforce.

Decades of debt

These are some of the pieces of equipment shipped from US factories during World War II. The Allies took decades to pay back their debts.

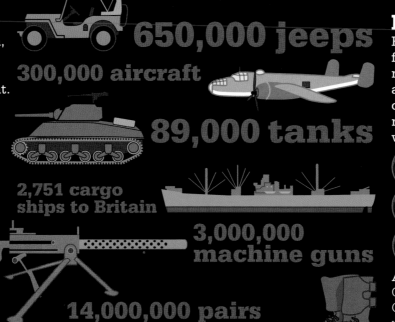

650,000 jeeps

300,000 aircraft

89,000 tanks

2,751 cargo ships to Britain

3,000,000 machine guns

14,000,000 pairs of boots to Russia

Horse sense

Horses were still important for transportation. Troops rode them, and they hauled artillery and other equipment on muddy and snowy routes that overwhelmed wheeled vehicles.

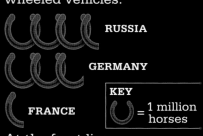

RUSSIA

GERMANY

FRANCE

KEY
= 1 million horses

At the front line

On the eastern front, most German artillery and supplies were horse drawn, and the Soviets had cavalry units.

War dead

Why did 2.5 percent of the world's population die? Death rates soared
when large regions, such as the Soviet Union and China, were invaded.
Many Holocaust victims came from eastern European countries, while
in divided nations, such as Yugoslavia, partisans fought one another.

KEY
MILITARY CASUALTIES
CIVILIAN CASUALTIES

FULL WIDTH = 10,000,000 CASUALTIES

SOVIET UNION: MILITARY 9,750,000 • CIVILIAN 13,650,000 • TOTAL 23,400,000

CHINA: MILITARY 3,500,000 • CIVILIAN 11,500,000 • TOTAL 15,000,000

GERMANY: MILITARY 5,527,000 • CIVILIAN 2,175,000 • TOTAL 7,702,000

POLAND: MILITARY 240,000 • CIVILIAN 5,480,000 • TOTAL 5,720,000

DUTCH EAST INDIES (INDONESIA): MILITARY 0 • CIVILIAN 3,500,000 • TOTAL 3,500,000

JAPAN: MILITARY 2,120,000 • CIVILIAN 750,000 • TOTAL 2,870,000

INDIA (BRITISH): MILITARY 87,000 • CIVILIAN 2,000,000 • TOTAL 2,087,000

YUGOSLAVIA: MILITARY 373,000 • CIVILIAN 990,000 • TOTAL 1,363,000

FRENCH INDOCHINA (VIETNAM): MILITARY 0 • CIVILIAN 1,125,000 • TOTAL 1,125,000

FULL WIDTH = 1,000,000 CASUALTIES

PHILIPPINES: MILITARY 57,000 • CIVILIAN 750,000 • TOTAL 807,000

ROMANIA: MILITARY 300,000 • CIVILIAN 500,000 • TOTAL 800,000

HUNGARY: MILITARY 300,000 • CIVILIAN 280,000 • TOTAL 580,000

FRANCE: MILITARY 217,600 • CIVILIAN 350,000 • TOTAL 567,600

GREECE: MILITARY 27,550 • CIVILIAN 535,000 • TOTAL 562,550

ITALY: MILITARY 301,400 • CIVILIAN 155,600 • TOTAL 457,000

UNITED KINGDOM: MILITARY 383,800 • CIVILIAN 67,100 • TOTAL 450,900

KOREA (JAPANESE): MILITARY 0 • CIVILIAN 430,500 • TOTAL 430,500

UNITED STATES: MILITARY 416,800 • CIVILIAN 1,700 • TOTAL 418,500

AUSTRIA: MILITARY 260,000 • CIVILIAN 120,000 • TOTAL 380,000

CZECHOSLOVAKIA: MILITARY 25,000 • CIVILIAN 300,000 • TOTAL 325,000

NETHERLANDS: MILITARY 17,000 • CIVILIAN 284,000 • TOTAL 301,000

BURMA: MILITARY 22,000 • CIVILIAN 250,000 • TOTAL 272,000

ABYSSINIA (ETHIOPIA): MILITARY 5,000 • CIVILIAN 95,000 • TOTAL 100,000

MALAYA (BRITISH): MILITARY 0 • CIVILIAN 100,000 • TOTAL 100,000

FINLAND: MILITARY 95,000 • CIVILIAN 2,000 • TOTAL 97,000

BELGIUM: MILITARY 12,100 • CIVILIAN 75,900 • TOTAL 88,000

SINGAPORE (BRITISH): MILITARY 0 • CIVILIAN 50,000 • TOTAL 50,000

Civilian fatalities
The huge numbers of

**There was
1 death every**

3 seconds

The postwar world [A new

The war ended, but suffering did not. Cities and towns were flattened, food was scarce, and millions had lost their homes. For people all over the world, recovery took decades. New countries and alliances formed, and the whole way the world was organized changed radically.

Postwar Europe

Stalin took control of Eastern Europe and the Baltic States to create a new Soviet-controlled empire. The US and the Soviet Union were the new "superpowers," but they did not get along. Their strained relationship was known as the Cold War; it became more dangerous starting in 1949, when the Soviets made an atomic bomb.

Different ideologies

From 1948, Europe was split into two blocs—the Communist East and the democratic, capitalist West. Each of the Eastern European states had a Communist government that was loyal to the USSR.

MAP KEY

■ Under Soviet control

State of Israel

The newly formed United Nations decided that Jews should have their own country. In May 1948, in a controversial move, it created the state of Israel by splitting the region of Palestine into Arab and Jewish states. Hundreds of thousands of surviving European Jews flooded in to help create the "Promised Land." Some Arabs in the region had to move out.

A new nation

The Declaration of Independence of the State of Israel was made on May 14 in Tel Aviv.

Divided city

By the late 1940s, Berlin, surrounded by Communist East Germany, was divided into the Communist East and the democratic West. The Berlin Wall literally divided the city between 1961 and 1989.

Home for heroes

Millions of soldiers returned home—by 1947, the number of armed forces from the United States alone shrank from 12 to 1.5 million. Many soldiers found it difficult to adjust to civilian life.

40 million:
the number of refugees in Europe when the war ended

Welcome home!

The *Queen Mary* docked in New York on June 20, 1945, carrying 15,642 troops, including 7,000 Canadians. About 435,000 GIs arrived home every month for the next year.

Hostile actions

The superpowers raced to develop deadly weapons. The US tested the first H-bomb in November 1952. The Soviet Union matched it in 1953.

The postwar world
With the major European nations weakened or needing aid after the war, countries that had been colonies left their European rulers or were encouraged to become independent. The age of empires was over. Communism gained influence as the balance of world power changed.

Berlin conquered
The Red Army entered Berlin on April 21, 1945. They looted buildings and attacked many civilians in revenge for the devastation caused by the Nazis.

China turns Communist
In 1949, Mao Tse-tung won a three-year civil war and largely isolated China until 1976.

Independent India
Mahatma Gandhi's Quit India campaign helped end British rule in August 1947. India and the new state of Pakistan became independent.

Changes in Japan
The Japanese emperor lost all political and military power in 1947. Japanese women voted for the first time in the 1948 elections.

1947
The American Marshall Plan pumped $13 billion into European countries to support industry and agriculture.

1949
On April 4, Western powers fearful of Communist threats formed the North Atlantic Treaty Organization (NATO), a political and military peacekeeping alliance.

1951
The European Coal and Steel Community, a stepping stone to the European Union, was founded to join countries in an economic union and to make war less likely.

PHOTOGRAPHY

1: akg-images; 2–3: Getty Images; 4–5 (background): Fotolia; 6: Library of Congress Prints and Photographs Division; 7l: Time & Life Pictures/Getty Images; 7cl: akg-images; 7cr: Getty Images; 7r: akg-images; 8–9: Getty Images; 10–11: Associated Press; 12l: Library of Congress; 12c: Associated Press; 12r: Roger Viollet/Getty Images; 14tl: Bettmann/Corbis/AP Images; 14tr: Pictorial Press Ltd/Alamy; 14bl: IAM/akg/World History Archive; 14br: akg-images/Interfoto; 15tr: BPK, Berlin/Art Resource; 15bl: Associated Press; 15br: Deutsches Bundesarchiv/Wikimedia Commons; 16tl: Associated Press; 16–17: Three Lions/Getty Images; 17tr, 17cl: Associated Press; 17bc: Thomas Reimer, Fotolia; 18–19 (all): Associated Press; 20 (Mussolini, Hitler): Associated Press; 20br: Time & Life Pictures/Getty Images; 21 (Stalin, Roosevelt): Associated Press; 21br: The Print Collector/Alamy; 23 (Hitler): US National Archives and Records Administration; 24–25: Roger Viollet/Getty Images; 26–27 (maps): Shutterstock; 26br, 27bl: Associated Press; 27bc: ITAR-TASS Photo Agency/Alamy; 28l: Time & Life Pictures/Getty Images; 28c: Dave Bartruff/Corbis; 30tl: IAM/akg/World History Archive; 30tr: Time & Life Pictures/Getty Images; 30bl, 30br: Associated Press; 31tr: Getty Images; 31bl: James King-Holmes/Bletchley Park Trust/Photo Researchers, Inc.; 31br, 32bc: Getty Images; 33b: Associated Press; 34–35: Time & Life Pictures/Getty Images; 36tl: Prisma Bildagentur AG/Alamy; 36c, 36bl, 36bc, 36–37: Jose Lasheras; 37tc: Jean Mounicq/Roger-Viollet/The Image Works; 37tr, 37br: Jose Lasheras; 38–39: Pictorial Press Ltd/Alamy; 39tl: Associated Press; 39tr: RIA Novosti/Alamy; 39c: National Firearms Museum; 40–41: RIA Novosti/Alamy; 42tr: Dave Bartruff/Corbis; 42bl: riekephotos/Shutterstock; 42–43: Imagno/Getty; 45: Photodynamx/Dreamstime; 46 (Land Army): Associated Press; 48tr: AF Archive/Alamy; 50cl: Science Source/Getty Images; 50c: United Archives GmbH/Alamy; 50–51 (Enigma): SSPL/Science Museum/Getty Images; 50–51 (ticker tape), 51tr, 51rc: Jose Lasheras; 51br: Wikimedia Commons; 52l: Library of Congress; 52c: Getty Images; 54tl: Library of Congress; 54tr: Editorial/Dreamstime; 54bl: UC Berkeley, Bancroft Library; 54br: akg-images; 55tl: Associated Press; 55tr: US Navy Photograph, National Archives; 55bl, 55br, 56–57: Library of Congress; 57r: National Archives; 58c, 58bl, 58bc, 58br: Stocktrek Images, Inc./Alamy; 58tr: akg-images; 58–59: Corbis; 59tl, 59tr: akg-images; 60–61: Library of Congress; 62bl: Tiono Sudihadi/Dreamstime; 62–63: Bettmann/Corbis; 63tr: Tiono Sudihadi/Dreamstime; 63br: Mary Evans Picture Library/Alamy; 64b: akg-images; 66–67: Getty Images; 67br: Bettmann/Corbis/AP Images; 68–69 (all): Jose Lasheras; 70bl: Wikimedia Commons; 70tc: Hulton Archive/Getty Images; 70tr: Gaius Cornelius/Wikimedia Commons; 70–71: Popperfoto/Getty Images; 71tl: National Archive; 72tr: US Air Force; 74bl: US Navy; 76–77: Associated Press; 78l: National Archives; 78r: Getty Images; 80tl: akg-images; 80tr: akg-images/ullstein bild; 80br: akg-images; 81tl: Glenn Berg; 81tr: akg-images; 81bl: Library and Archives Canada; 81br, 82tl: Associated Press; 82–83, 83c: National Archives; 83tr: Jose Lasheras; 84tl: ClassicStock.com/SuperStock; 84 (grenade): Mccool/Dreamstime; 84 (mine, rifle): Jose Lasheras; 86cl: British Army; 87t, 87ct, 87cb, 87b: Jose Lasheras; 88c: Glenn Berg; 88br: Getty Images; 89tl: Associated Press; 89 (background): Time & Life Pictures/Getty Images; 90l: Popperfoto/Getty Images; 90c, 90r: akg-images; 92tl, 92tr: National Archives; 92bl: Library of Congress; 92br: akg-images; 93tr: Library of Congress; 93bl: Trinity Mirror/Mirrorpix/Alamy; 93br: Photo Researchers, Inc.; 94–95: Popperfoto/Getty Images; 96c: The Print Collector/Alamy; 96tr: Associated Press; 98l: akg-images; 98–99: Getty Images; 99bc, 100–101: akg-images; 101r: National Archives; 104cl: Mishella/Dreamstime; 104bl: Bettmann/Corbis/AP Images; 104cr: Erik1977/Dreamstime; 104br: Bettmann/Corbis/AP Images; 105tl: Georgios Kollidas/iStockphoto; 105tcl: Wikimedia Commons; 105tcr: Associated Press; 105b: ITAR-TASS Photo Agency/Alamy; 108: Jose Lasheras.

ARTWORK

15tl, 26bl, 33c: Anders Lejczak; 28r, 31tl, 32c, 48–49, 52r, 72–73, 78c, 84–85, 93tl: Tim Loughhead; all other artwork: Scholastic.

COVER

Front cover: Getty Images. Back cover: (tr) Tim Loughhead; (computer monitor) Manaemedia/Dreamstime.

Key to symbols in **More here** columns

Keywords for web searches

Suggested reading

Watch on TV, on DVD, or online

Listen to songs or recordings

Visit exciting places

Great things to do

Mini-glossary

Credits and
acknowledgments